Elite • 269

# US Tank Tactics in World War II

STEVEN J. ZALOGA

ILLUSTRATED BY STEVE NOON

Series editor Nick Reynolds

OSPREY PUBLISHING
Bloomsbury Publishing Plc
Kemp House, Chawley Park, Cumnor Hill, Oxford OX2 9PH, UK
Bloomsbury Publishing Ireland Limited,
29 Earlsfort Terrace, Dublin 2, D02 AY28, Ireland
Bloomsbury Publishing Inc.
1359 Broadway, 12th Floor, New York, NY 10018, USA
E-mail: info@ospreypublishing.com
**www.ospreypublishing.com**

OSPREY is a trademark of Osprey Publishing Ltd

First published in Great Britain in 2026



A catalog record for this book is available from the British Library.

ISBN: PB 9781472871329; eBook 9781472871336;
ePDF 9781472871305; XML 9781472871312

26 27 28 29 30 10 9 8 7 6 5 4 3 2 1

Index by Mark Swift
Typeset by Lumina Datamatics Ltd
Printed by Repro India Ltd.

MIX
Paper
FSC FSC® C047271

Osprey Publishing supports the Woodland Trust, the UK's leading woodland conservation charity.

To find out more about our authors and books visit **www.ospreypublishing.com**. Here you will find extracts, author interviews, details of forthcoming events and the option to sign up for our newsletter.

For product safety related questions contact productsafety@bloomsbury.com

## Author's note

This book examines the origins and evolution of US Army tank tactics in World War II. For the US Army, tank combat in the European Theater of Operations (ETO) was by far the largest battle zone, constituting about 77 percent of wartime tank losses compared to about 10 percent for Italy and the Pacific and 3 percent for North Africa. As a result, the special focus of this book is on US Army tank employment in the ETO.

Tactics are inextricably linked to army organization. For readers wishing a more in-depth look at US tank unit organization during World War II, there are three volumes by the author in the Osprey Battle Orders series: *US Armored Divisions: The European Theater of Operations, 1944–45* (2004); *US Tank and Tank Destroyer Battalions in the ETO 1944–45* (2005); and *US Armored Units in the North African and Italian Campaigns 1942–45* (2006). The contentious issue of the interplay between US Army tank and tank-destroyer doctrine is avoided in this book due to lack of space; it is covered in the Battle Orders series. All photographs in this book are from US government archives, primarily the US Army's Signal Corps collections.

## Artist's note

Readers may care to note that the original paintings from which the color plates in this book were prepared are available for private sale.
All reproduction copyright whatsoever is retained by the publishers.
All inquiries should be addressed to:

https://www.steve-noon.co.uk/

The publishers regret that they can enter into no correspondence upon this matter.

Title-page photograph: The MacArthur reforms of 1931 permitted the cavalry to mechanize. Here, M1A1 combat cars of Troop F, 13th Cavalry Regiment (Mechanized) pass by a column of halftrack-towed 75mm howitzers of the 68th Field Artillery Battalion during the Third Army Maneuvers on the Texas–Louisiana border in May 1940.

# CONTENTS

# US TANK TACTICS IN WORLD WAR II

## ORIGINS OF US TANK TACTICS

The first US Army experience with tanks was during World War I. In 1918, the American Expeditionary Forces (AEF) in France deployed two battalions of French-supplied Renault FT light tanks and one battalion of British-supplied Mark V heavy tanks. Early US tank tactics were strongly influenced by the French Army because most tactical training in 1918 was done under the guidance of French officers. The basic tactics were outlined in a manual released in December 1918 by the AEF entitled "Tanks: Organization and Tactics." These guidelines remained the basis for US Army tactical doctrine in the 1920s and 1930s and so are worth quoting in detail:

> Tanks are essentially an Infantry supporting arm or an auxiliary to the Infantry and only on rare occasions should they act independently. Tanks provide a means of advancing Infantry weapons or Infantry supporting weapons under artificial cover invulnerable to small arms, to positions from which they can materially affect the hostile fire and assist in the establishment of the fire superiority necessary to the advance of the Infantry. At the same time, tanks are of advantage in making paths through wire obstacles for the advance of the accompanying Infantry. These are the essential functions of the tank and its tactical employment should be based [on these].
>
> Tanks do not relieve the Infantry of the necessity of maneuvering and fighting. Infantry supported by Tanks, will still have to use the rifle to gain that fire superiority which is necessary to enable it to advance and to capture or destroy the hostile forces with which it may come in contact. The Infantry that is assisted by Tanks will be prepared to aid any Tank that is temporarily disabled and will not abandon a disabled Tank to the enemy …
>
> Tanks should not be employed singly. They should never be employed in groups of less than two and not, as a general rule, in groups of less than a platoon … Tanks are well suited to operate in co-operation with Infantry against villages, machine gun nests or strong points which are not directly supported by artillery fire or whose artillery fire may be neutralized, and to operate with the Infantry in cleaning up areas passed over by assaulting troops.
>
> On rare occasions, the military situation may permit of the assignment of an independent mission to Tank units, as in attack of

A 6-ton light tank of the 1st Tank Company, 424th Infantry Regiment (Light Tanks) taking part in summer maneuvers in La Tourette Park, Staten Island, New York in August 1934. This was a US copy of the Renault FT light tank.

> the enemy in a disorganized retreat, for the purpose of increasing disorder or cutting off his retreat; or when his main line of resistance has been broken and when his artillery is inactive, an attack upon his infantry reserves, thus preventing the enemy organizing opposition to the advance of our Infantry. Under such circumstances Tanks should be used en masse with boldness and aggressiveness.
>
> Tanks being a supporting arm of the Infantry, their formation for attack should be adapted to the formation for the Infantry. Whether Tanks shall precede or follow the Infantry in the attack will depend upon the military situation as may be determined by a complete estimate of the situation.

These basic tactical guidelines remained the rule for the next two decades. One of the basic premises was that tanks were limited to supporting the infantry and had no independent role of their own with only rare exceptions. Following the war, the US Congress abolished the Tank Corps and subordinated tanks to the Infantry branch. The majority of tanks served in companies attached to the regular infantry divisions, with another 15 light tank companies scattered around the country with National Guard infantry units. In the view of American political and military leaders, the 1914–18 conflict had represented the "war to end all wars," implying that that there would be no future involvement in high-intensity conflict in Europe. This meant that the US Army would probably return to its usual role as a frontier constabulary on the Mexican border and in the colonies such as the Philippines where tanks were of little use. Tank production was constricted by a lack of funds so the US Army relied on World War I-era tanks through the early 1930s.

In 1927, Secretary of War Dwight F. Davis witnessed Britain's Experimental Mechanised Force during an official visit to the country. On his return, he instructed the US Army to conduct a similar exercise, and this began in the summer of 1928 at Camp Meade, Maryland. Although the exercise was praised by some US Army leaders, the Infantry and Cavalry branches saw no need for a permanent Mechanized Force and it was disbanded in 1931. Under the new army chief-of-staff, General Douglas MacArthur, both the Infantry and Cavalry branches were authorized to undertake mechanization on their

Early tanks were not very durable and relied on tank transporters for any long-distance marches. This is a column of the Mechanized Force from Fort Eustis, Virginia, consisting of Tank Carrier Six Wheels (TC-SW) with T1E1 and 6-ton light tanks aboard, crossing the James River Bridge, Virginia, during 1931 maneuvers.

own paths. The Cavalry was not allowed tanks under the 1920 Congressional edict, but this restriction was avoided by designating the cavalry tanks as "combat cars." The Cavalry branch became the hotbed of US Army mechanization in the mid-1930s while the Infantry branch still restricted tanks to a supporting role.

The eruption of wars in Europe and Asia in the 1930s began to raise the possibility of a new global conflict. The Spanish Civil War (1936–39) was the first war to see extensive tank use by both sides. The Second Sino-Japanese War (1937–45) between China and Japan saw an increasing use of tanks, though predominantly by the Japanese. The US Army took notice of the role of tanks in these conflicts, but information was scarce and the "lessons" of these wars were distorted to fit the preconceptions of various US Army leaders.

The outbreak of war in Europe in 1939 forced the US Army to begin a substantial modernization program on the presumption that the United States would eventually be dragged into the growing conflagration. The Cavalry branch proposed expanding the 7th Cavalry Brigade (Mechanized) into a full mechanized division. The Infantry branch consolidated its scattered divisional tank companies into the 68th Infantry Regiment (Tank) at Fort Benning, Georgia, and in the winter of 1939/40 began to organize a Provisional Tank Brigade. By the spring of 1940, the US Army deployed two mechanized cavalry regiments, five light tank battalions in the 67th and 68th Infantry (Tanks), one medium tank company, and 13 National Guard divisional tank companies.

In the wake of the lightning German victory in Poland, on October 17, 1939, the US Army's chiefs of Infantry and Cavalry branches, Major General George A. Lynch and Major General John K. Herr respectively, met to discuss the possible organization of the first US Army armored divisions. Lynch had extremely narrow views of the value of tanks, feeling that they were only useful in supporting the infantry by destroying enemy machine-gun nests. He deferred to the cavalry to lobby for deeper mechanization and suggested that all tanks under 10 tons go to the mechanized cavalry, and that only tanks over 10 tons, namely the new M2 and M2A1 medium tanks, should remain with the infantry.

Frustrated by the conservative approaches of the Infantry and Cavalry, the War Department ordered the branches to cooperate in testing a provisional mechanized force in the May 1940 maneuvers including the 6th Infantry Regiment (Motorized), the Provisional Tank Brigade, and 7th Cavalry Brigade. Various combinations of units were employed during the war games. At one point, this embryonic armored division trounced the 1st Cavalry Division. After the war games, a post-maneuver conference was conducted, headed by the War Department's chief of operations, Brigadier General Frank M. Andrews. The officers present concluded that the future of US Army mechanization should be taken out of the stultifying control of the Infantry and Cavalry branches' chiefs and placed under the control of a new "non-sectarian" organization.

# TANK TACTICS IN 1940–41

The shocking defeat of France in May–June 1940 provided the final catalyst for change. Major General Andrews pushed the US Army chief-of-staff, General George C. Marshall, to create a new force to organize and train the new mechanized elements. The Armored Force was created at Fort Knox, Kentucky, on July 10, 1940, barely three weeks after the French defeat. The name was chosen as a compromise – the infantry didn't want the cavalry term "mechanized" used and the cavalry felt the same way about the term "tank," which its officers associated with the infantry. The Armored Force was not a branch coequal to the Infantry and Cavalry branches because it had not received Congressional approval. Regardless, it functioned like a branch until the 1950 Army Organization Act formally established Armor as a permanent branch. Command of the Armored Force was handed over to a cavalry general, Major General Adna R. Chaffee, Jr., long one of the most forceful advocates of US Army mechanization.

The new force absorbed all the Infantry's tank units and the Cavalry's various mechanized units as well. The initial organization began with the formation of two armored divisions: the 1st Armored Division based around the 1st and 13th Cavalry Regiments, and the 2d Armored Division based around the 67th and 68th Infantry Regiments. The 1st Battalion, 67th Armored Regiment, was converted into the separate 70th GHQ Reserve Tank Battalion at Fort Meade, Maryland. The numerous separate tank companies in the National Guard were mobilized under Federal control and used to form the 191st–194th separate tank battalions. Two of these were used to form the Provisional Tank Group that was deployed to the Philippines in the fall of 1941. The new 751st–760th battalions were formed in June 1941, the 751st–755th as medium tank battalions equipped with the new M3 medium tank, and the 756th–760th in the usual light tank configuration, equipped with the new M3 light tank. By the end of 1941, the number of General Headquarters (GHQ) tank battalions had increased to 15.

The organization and tactics of the Armored Force were strongly influenced by German practices. As in the case of the Wehrmacht, US armored

The 192d Tank Battalion was created in November 1940 from National Guard tank companies from Wisconsin, Illinois, Ohio, and Kentucky. Its M2A2 light tanks are shown here at the Second Army maneuvers in Arkansas in September 1941. Shortly after, the battalion was sent to the Philippines where it was re-equipped with M3 light tanks before seeing combat in December 1941.

divisions were tank-heavy. The original organization of the US armored division in 1940 was patterned on the prewar German model with an armored brigade of three tank regiments, a mechanized infantry regiment, an armored artillery regiment, and supporting engineer and mechanized cavalry reconnaissance battalions. As in the case of the Wehrmacht, the US Army established Armored Corps headquarters to manage the armored divisions. Tentative steps were also undertaken to create motorized infantry divisions, based on the German example. Separate tank battalions were few in number with tanks heavily concentrated in armored divisions. The traditional role of tanks for direct infantry support was viewed as antediluvian and a reflection of the failed practices of the interwar years.

US tactical doctrine was shaped by the predominant role of cavalry officers in the senior ranks, including such well-known figures as Major General George S. Patton, Jr., who would eventually command the 2d Armored Division. The principal tactical role of the armored divisions was the exploitation of the breakthrough once infantry divisions had penetrated enemy defenses. The armored divisions were explicitly discouraged from a breakthrough mission. The small number of separate tank battalions were directed by a new type of brigade headquarters called the armored group that would have tactical control over several tank battalions to engage in maneuver missions, taking them away from their traditional infantry support role.

The new armored formations underwent several structural modifications based on the lessons from the fall 1941 war games. The Armored Force recognized that the original armored division organization was gravely flawed. Its striking echelon consisted of a brigade consisting of two light tank regiments and one medium tank regiment supported by an armored artillery regiment. The support echelon contained the armored division's armored infantry regiment and engineers. The armored division was too tank-centric, however, containing eight battalions of tanks but only two each of infantry and artillery for a ratio of 8:2:2. The new March 1942 organization dropped the armored brigade headquarters, cut one armored regiment, and added one infantry and one artillery battalion. This brought the balance to 6:3:3. More importantly, the war games revealed the need for combined-arms tactics paralleling the German *Kampfgruppe* (combat group). Unlike the German practice of extemporized combat groups, the US Army decided to institute a formal headquarters to manage the combined-arms teams. This was originally called the "combat team" through 1942 and it eventually crystallized into the "combat command." The 1942 division had two combat commands: Combat Command A (CCA) and Combat Command B (CCB). These headquarters did not have battalions regularly assigned to them; their organization was temporary and contingent on the mission.

The Armored Force took over the cavalry's mantle as the arm of maneuver in the US Army. Here, an M2A4 light tank of the 67th Armored Regiment, 2d Armored Division, passes a column of Troop A, 9th Cavalry Regiment, during the GHQ Maneuvers in Louisiana in September 1941.

Douglas A-20 Havoc light bombers pass overhead as a column of M3 medium tanks of the 1st Armored Division overrun a 37mm antitank gun position on a road in Castor, Louisiana, on September 11, 1941, during the Louisiana Maneuvers. These maneuvers were choreographed and often unrealistic, but led to a number of important changes in armored organization and tactics.

# THE BASICS: TANKS, TACTICS, AND ORGANIZATION

US armored units had a relatively small assortment of tank types during World War II. By far the most common type in the initial years of the war was the light tank. This was because the US Army felt that a light tank could accomplish the principal mission of supporting infantry. The main threat to infantry was the enemy machine-gun nest, and light tanks could deal with this threat in terms of armor and firepower. The typical light tanks of the mid-1930s were armed with light machine guns and .50-caliber heavy machine guns and protected with armor up to 1in thick. An additional factor favoring light tanks was the resistance by the US Army's Corps of Engineers to tanks over 10 tons because existing tactical bridging could not support heavier tanks. As a related issue, tanks heavier than 10 tons could not be easily transported overseas due to the limitations of US Navy cranes and small craft capable of delivering tanks to the shore.

This began to change after 1936 due to the lessons of the Spanish Civil War. The appearance of German 37mm and Soviet 45mm antitank guns threatened the viability of the light tank on the battlefield. As these weapons began to proliferate, tanks became heavier. This was evident in Europe where French infantry light tanks began to be protected by armor of about 40mm, raising their weight to about 15 tons. French cavalry tanks armed with 47mm guns began approaching 20 tons. Likewise, the Wehrmacht began shifting to a new generation of tanks weighing 20 tons or more.

## Light tanks

The US Army responded to the lessons of the Spanish Civil War with the M2A4 and M3 light tanks, armed with a 37mm M5 and 37mm M6 gun respectively. The 37mm gun was adequate to deal with contemporary light tanks while still being capable of firing a worthwhile high-explosive projectile. The main difference between the M2A4 and M3 was thicker frontal armor of 1½in on the M3. This was about as heavy as the chassis could manage without requiring a complete redesign of the tank. By 1941, the M3 was the most numerous tank in US Army service, and remained so well into 1942. Besides its use in the armored divisions in early 1942, the M3 equipped ten of the 15 separate tank battalions. Older light tanks, such as the prewar M2A2, were still used in separate tank battalions in early 1942 but were withdrawn to training units as the M3 became available. The M3 and M3A1 light tanks saw extensive combat use in 1942–43 in the Pacific Theater of Operations (PTO) and North Africa.

| US Army tank strength, February 27, 1942 | | | |
|---|---|---|---|
| M1, M2 light tanks | 421 | M2, M2A1 medium tanks | 93 |
| M2A4 light tanks | 268 | M3 medium tanks | 836 |
| M3 light tanks | 1,665 | ***Medium tanks, subtotal*** | ***929*** |
| ***Light tanks, subtotal*** | ***2,354*** | **Total** | **3,283** |

The M3's Continental radial engine was in high demand for aircraft, prompting the US Army to develop an alternative powered by Cadillac automobile engines. This was the M5 light tank and it entered production in April 1942. It first saw service in November 1942 during the Operation *Torch* landings in North Africa. By the summer of 1943, the M3A1 had been withdrawn from front-line US Army service in the Mediterranean Theater of Operations (MTO), replaced by the M5 and M5A1 light tanks. The M3A1 remained in limited combat service with US Marine Corps tank battalions into 1944, however, often as flamethrower tanks. The M5 was followed in September 1942 by the M5A1, which introduced an enlarged turret that moved the radio from the hull to the turret bustle. This was based on a British request but marked a general trend in US tanks to shift the radio to a position adjacent to the commander. This was the most common light tank in US service in 1944–45.

The sole combat use of the M2A4 light tank in combat during World War II was by the US Marine Corps' 1st Tank Battalion on Guadalcanal in 1942.

Combat experiences in Tunisia in early 1943 led to extensive criticism of the M3 and M5 as being too weakly armored and armed. In June 1943, Lieutenant General Omar N. Bradley, commander of II Corps, and Lieutenant General George S. Patton, Jr.,

An M3A1 light tank of the 758th Tank Battalion taking part in the September 1942 Tennessee Maneuvers with the Blue Army. This was the first of three segregated African American tank battalions. It was deployed to Italy and served in combat with the 92d Infantry Division.

commander of I Armored Corps (Reinforced), issued a directive that light tanks were only to be used for reconnaissance and flank security in view of their weakness in dealing with contemporary German tanks and antitank guns.

The US Army intended to replace the M3 light tank with the M7 light tank in March 1941. This was originally a 16-ton design armed with a 37mm gun and enough armor to withstand German 37mm antitank gun fire. As the war continued, however, German antitank guns continued to increase in power. Additional armor was added to the M7 design, and its firepower was increased to a 57mm T2 gun and finally to a 75mm M3 gun. In the process, the M7's weight increased from 16 tons to 28 tons, and its automotive performance suffered accordingly. Production of the M7 commenced in December 1942, but the Armored Force categorically refused to accept the vehicle, arguing with the Ordnance branch that it had failed to meet its design objectives. The M7 had become a medium tank that was heavier than the M4 Sherman medium tank but inferior in most respects. M7 production ended, leaving the US Army without a new light tank.

A follow-on program resulted in the M24 light tank. This had the same powertrain as the M5A1, but it was armed with a 75mm M6 gun. Production began in late 1944 and the M24 first entered combat around Christmas 1944 during the Ardennes campaign. Although lightly armored, it was a thoroughly modern design and arguably the best light tank of World War II.

The M2 medium tank of 1940 was a testament to the Infantry branch's obsession with machine guns, boasting no fewer than eight .30-caliber M1919 machine guns but only one puny 37mm M3 gun. The M2 entered production around the same time as the Soviet T-34 medium tank.

## Medium tanks

In response to the threat of war, the US Army adopted its first modern medium tank, the M2, in 1940. This tank was archaic in armament and design, however, and as a consequence was built in small numbers. By early 1942, all had been relegated to training units at the Armored Force School at Fort Knox. In the wake of the defeat of France in mid-1940, the US Army began to adopt a modernized derivative, the M3 medium tank. This used a hybrid armament consisting of an M2/M3 75mm dual-purpose gun in the hull, a 37mm M5/M6 antitank gun in the turret, and multiple .30-caliber M1919A4 machine guns. The M3 gradually equipped the new armored divisions as well as five new separate tank battalions created in June 1941.

The Armored Force was unhappy with the hybrid armament of the M3 and preferred a more conventional design with a 75mm gun in a turret.

"Buturlinovka III," the M3 medium tank of Captain Peter Meshkoff, commander of Co. B, 752d Tank Battalion, on exercise on Perham Down, Wiltshire, England, on December 6, 1942. The battalion was re-equipped with M4 medium tanks before it was committed to combat in Italy in January 1944.

Medium tank battalions were issued six 105mm M4 assault guns for indirect-fire assault. These resembled the normal M4 medium tank but were fitted with a 105mm M4 howitzer instead of the usual 75mm M3 gun. This is an M4 (105mm) assault gun of the HQ Company, 15th Tank Battalion, 6th Armored Division, near Troisvierges, Luxembourg, on January 24, 1945, at the conclusion of the Ardennes fighting.

This emerged as the M4 medium tank in February 1942. The M4 gradually replaced the M3 in the Armored Force as production permitted. The majority of M3 medium tanks, about 70 percent, were shipped to Britain and the Soviet Union via the Lend-Lease program. Owing to the crisis in North Africa, the re-equipment of the 1st Armored Division in 1942 from the M3 to the M4 was halted to provide more M4 Sherman medium tanks to Britain. The re-equipment program resumed in late 1942 so that by the time the 1st Armored Division was deployed in combat in November 1942 in North Africa, it had been completely re-equipped with M4s except for one battalion still equipped with M3s. The 751st Tank Battalion deployed to North Africa in early 1943 also had M3s. After the heavy US tank losses during the Kasserine Pass fighting in February 1943, some M3s were used to make up for losses. The limited use of the M3 in North Africa in 1942–43 was its only combat use by the US Army in World War II except for a company of M3A5 medium tanks of the 193d Tank Battalion that saw combat on Makin Atoll in the PTO in November 1943.

When first introduced into service in 1942, the M4 medium tank was widely regarded as one of the world's best tanks with excellent armor and firepower. These accolades gradually faded, however, due to the appearance of better German antitank guns and more powerful tanks such as the Tiger and Panther. The US Army initially discounted the Tiger threat because it was encountered in such small numbers in North Africa, Sicily, and Italy in 1942–43. When the Panther first appeared in 1943, it also was dismissed as another rare German heavy tank.

A program had been underway since 1942 to rearm the M4 with a more powerful 76mm gun, but this was rejected by the Armored Force until late 1943. When the first M4A1(76mm) medium tanks arrived in Britain in April 1944 prior to the D-Day landings, no tank units wanted them, because there was no need envisioned for their more powerful gun. To obtain its better high-velocity antitank performance, the new gun had inferior high-explosive performance. It was not until the summer of 1944, when the Panther was first encountered in large numbers, that the US Army appreciated the growing shortcomings of the M4's armament. Some hasty

The means of disseminating US Army tactical doctrine for the Armored Force was through publication of field manuals in the FM 17 series such as these from the author's collection.

improvements were made including new High-Velocity Armor Piercing (HVAP) ammunition. A successor to the M4, the M26 Pershing, did not appear until February 1945 and in very small numbers. Fortunately for the US Army, the German tank threat had been crushed in the Ardennes campaign, and collapsed in 1945.

## Crew drill

The most basic level of US tank tactics was called crew drill. This training took place after individual tank crewmen had been trained in their basic tasks and was intended to prepare the crew to work as a team in operating the tank. The basic guidelines for crew drill were established under the January 1942 field manual FM 17-5 "Armored Force Drill."

US tank crews in World War II were typically four men in a light tank and five men in a medium tank. The basic four-man crew in a light tank consisted of a tank commander, gunner, driver, and bow gunner. The medium tank had an additional crewman serving as a dedicated loader; on the light tank the tank commander doubled as the loader. Tank crews were usually cross-trained in the tasks of other crew members in order to provide redundancy in the event of crew casualties in combat. The seniority of the crew was usually in the order of tank commander, gunner, driver, because these required the most extensive training and experience.

The primary crew drill was called crew control and consisted of standardized terminology for the crew to interact using the tank's internal intercom system. Inside the tank, the crewmen wore tankers helmets

The crew of "Cowboy," an M4A3 medium tank of the 5th Armored Division, load ammunition into their tank during field training in the United States in 1943.

that included headphones and a throat microphone that connected into an intercom box inside the tank. After instruction on the operation of the intercom system in the tank, the crew was then trained on a series of standardized commands and replies. These were short and clear to make certain that the crew understood the commander's instructions in the heat of battle.

| **Crew drill, M4 medium tank engaging a target** | | |
|---|---|---|
| **Crewman** | **Instruction** | **Explanation** |
| Commander to gunner | Gunner … Traverse right | Initial instructions for traversing turret |
| Commander to gunner | Steady on | Halting the traverse |
| Commander to gunner | Truck | Identifying the target |
| Commander to gunner | Two hundred | Range in yards for the gunner to input super-elevation in the gun controls |
| Commander to loader | Loader … HE | Type of ammunition, in this case, High Explosive |
| Commander to gunner | Fire! | Fire on target |

The crew of "Hawkeye," an M4 medium tank of Co. H, 3/66th Armored, 2d Armored Division, conducting crew drills in England in the spring of 1944 prior to the Normandy landings. The tanker on the right is loading an assortment of grenades while the two crewmen on the left are loading 75mm gun ammunition.

Dismounted drill involved the crew taking up positions outside the tank for instruction by the tank commander or other officers. Service of the piece was periodic instruction in the operation of the weapons on the tank. Besides basic service of the piece, the crew also underwent extensive gunnery training on tank firing ranges. Crew evacuation was training on how to best evacuate the tank as well as techniques for removing wounded crewmen. Inspection and maintenance outlined the role of each crewman in daily maintenance work on the tank as well as common field repairs such as repairing a broken track, cleaning air filters, replenishing fuel and oil, and so on. Destruction of materiel was a drill to instruct the crew how to destroy the most vital parts of their tank to prevent it from falling into enemy hands in an operable condition.

**A**

**PATTON'S ARM: THE TANK MACHINE GUN**

Lieutenant General George S. Patton, Jr., was an enthusiastic proponent of tank machine guns. During World War II, he wrote letters to Ordnance encouraging the addition of more machine guns on tanks. One of his young disciples, Brigadier General Bruce C. Clarke, explained why: "I told my men that the greatest thing on the tank was a free .50 cal. in the hands of the tank commander. We were not able to fight from tanks with the tank commander buttoned up – that has never been successfully done. [Buttoned up] he can't hear or see and so pretty soon he unbuttons. Now if he's got a free .50 cal machine gun, all he has to do is press his thumb and he can pick out a dangerous spot. It may be a bazooka flash or something. He can throw a burst there without even thinking about giving an order."

# TANK UNIT ORGANIZATION AND TACTICS 1940–43

US tank tactics were formally issued for training and operational use as field manuals, approved by the Secretary of War and released by the US Army Adjutant General. The basic Armored Force field manual, FM 17-10 "Tactics and Techniques," was released in March 1942, and provided a thumbnail description of the basic employment of tank units:

> The characteristics of Armored Force units are:
> Mobility—All combat units are mounted in armored motor vehicles.
> Fire power—Through a multiplicity of weapons mounted on the vehicles.
> Armor protection—All combat vehicles are protected by armor of varying thickness, capable of withstanding at least rifle fire.
> Shock action—Accomplished by the combination of the other characteristics and by the weight and crushing power of the major vehicles.
> The operations of components of the Armored Force may, at various times or simultaneously, involve:
> The attachment of GHQ tank battalions and groups to infantry, cavalry, and armored divisions or corps.
> The grouping of armored divisions, corps, or GHQ tank groups with other corps or field armies for combined operations.
> The employment, by the field or theater commander, of armored divisions and corps on independent or semi-independent missions without reinforcing logistical means, or additional supporting troops other than combat and reconnaissance aviation.
> Operation as *task forces* wherein armored divisions or corps or, at times GHQ reserve tank units, are teamed with motorized divisions, antitank battalions, antiaircraft automatic weapons battalions, and GHQ engineer, maintenance, and supply units, closely supported by combat aviation, parachute, and other troops transported by air.

The different role of armored divisions compared to separate tank battalions was outlined in the October 1942 edition of FM 17-30 "Tank Platoon":

> The mission of tanks in the armored division is to attack and destroy vital hostile installations such as command posts, communication centers, supply installations, reserves, and artillery. The mission of tanks in the separate tank battalions is to assist infantry, cavalry, or motorized divisions to advance by destroying hostile machine guns, personnel, and vital installations.

Although US Army tank tactics shared much in common at various levels of organization, tactical doctrine was dependent on the size and role of the tank units. Each of the major categories of tank unit tactics in the 1941–43 period are outlined below.

## The tank platoon

The basic US Army tank tactical unit was the tank platoon. A US tank platoon in World War II was five tanks. The platoon was led by a lieutenant, while the remaining four tanks were commanded by sergeants. Platoon tactics were outlined in FM 17-30, released in October 1942 and revised in July 1944. The tactics were organized under six sections: training (general, terrain, weapons and ammunition); control, orders, and reconnaissance; marches; security; offensive action; and defense. Tank platoon tactics were the basic building block of US Army tank tactics. So, it is worthwhile to recount the basic outline of tank platoon tactics found in FM 17-30:

The US Army formed several independent tank companies with Marmon Herrington T14 (CTLS-4TAY) and T16 (CTLS-4TAC) light tanks for coastal defense in Alaska. This is a T14 of the 602d Independent Tank Company, formerly Co. B, 35th Tank Company, of the Missouri National Guard, serving with the 135th Infantry Regiment on Umnak Island off the Alaskan coast in 1942.

> The tank platoon is the smallest tank battle unit. It normally operates as part of the tank company. However, it may operate as an independent unit as advance, flank, or rear guard or on similar missions. Tanks operate by surprise, fire and maneuver, and in mass. The violation of these fundamentals will lead to ineffectual effort and perhaps disaster. Surprise is gained by striking the enemy at an unexpected time, from an unexpected direction, with all strength possible. Speed of movement, use of covered approaches, and coordination of fires assist in gaining surprise. *Seek to surprise the enemy but do not let yourself be surprised. Give the enemy credit for being as capable as yourself. Do not underestimate his ability. Do not become careless. Expect the unexpected and be prepared for it.*
>
> An advancing unit is covered by the fire of weapons in stationary position. This is important as the tank in the open is not only extremely vulnerable but movement, dust, and restricted vision make the locating of new targets extremely difficult. Tanks in defiladed position can quickly locate and promptly bring fire upon hostile weapons that fire upon the advancing tanks. This procedure of fire and movement may be by section, platoon, or company. Concentrate effort. Do not waste strength on numerous unimportant targets. Strike on a key position with all power that can be mustered. If this falls, others may then be taken. If effort is made on several positions, the enemy may easily destroy you by concentrating successively on each attacking element.
>
> Coordination of effort, that is, timing of all elements, is essential. An uncoordinated effort violates the fundamental of the use of mass. Therefore, in attack, time the movement of the tanks and the opening of fire by supporting weapons or supporting tanks so that maximum effect is obtained. Teamwork is essential. In order to obtain success in battle, leaders must exercise initiative and act aggressively. A small force acting under direction of an aggressive, alert, leader can overcome a much larger force whose leader is slow and nonaggressive. Do not let the enemy have time to get set. Conversely, do not rush headlong into battle with no plan of action. Think clearly, give clear orders, *then* act fast. Seek to strike the enemy where he is weak in antitank defense. Do not drive headlong against strong antitank defense. Bypass it or call for assistance to reduce it.

A tank attack will usually be launched in three echelons, each echelon in a series of waves. The first echelon of attack, preceded by neutralization by combat aviation and artillery, if available, is directed against the antitank defenses, artillery, command posts, and other rear installations. Tank platoons of this echelon destroy first the enemy antitank defenses and second, enemy artillery. They attack enemy infantry only when hindered by it in fulfilling their primary missions.

The platoons of the second echelon follow the first echelon at such distance that the enemy will not have time to re form his antitank defenses. These platoons destroy hostile automatic guns and personnel and clear the way for the advance of infantry. Antitank guns passed over by the first echelon must be silenced by the leading waves of the second echelon.

The tank platoons of the third echelon advance with the infantry, destroy hostile machine guns passed over by the second echelon, and hostile personnel. The mission of this echelon is to assist the advance of the infantry. They may lead the infantry attack if resistance is still heavy. If resistance has been broken by the first two echelons, tanks of the third echelon will follow the infantry, prepared to attack isolated resistance as necessary. These tanks also protect the infantry from counterattack, particularly of mechanized forces.

## The tank company

A US Army tank company typically consisted of three tank platoons, a headquarters section, maintenance section, and an administration, maintenance, and supply (AMS) section. Companies were either light or medium, and thus equipped with M3/M5 light tanks or M3/M4 medium tanks. The HQ section consisted of two tanks for the commander and executive officer and a jeep; after the 1943 reorganization, an assault gun was added to the section. Assault guns were derived from light and medium tanks, but fitted with a howitzer for indirect fire in place of the usual high-velocity tank gun. The maintenance section consisted of a jeep for the section leader, a halftrack, and a tank recovery vehicle. The maintenance and supply section had a 2½-ton truck and trailer.

The tank company tactics outlined in FM 17-32 "The Tank Company, Light and Medium," released in August 1942, covered many of the same basic tactical principles outlined in FM 17-30, and so will not be repeated here. The basic approach to tank company tactics emphasized the US Army's combined-arms approach, noting that tank companies would often be reinforced with elements of other units:

**B**

**TANK PLATOON WEDGE FORMATION IN THE ADVANCE**

The Armored Force drill offered various types of formations for movement for a tank platoon. A tank platoon line formation was generally about 200–800yd wide depending on the circumstances. A platoon tank column was 200–800yd long. A wedge formation was a common offensive formation and had the platoon leader in the lead with two sections of two tanks each on either flank. FM 17-30 "Tank Platoon" notes that the wedge formation "affords good fire power to the front and either flank. It is easy to control as far as direction is concerned. However, its fire power is difficult to control due to the fact that the platoon leader is not in a position to see his sections readily." An alternative was the inverted wedge with the commander in the rear. FM 17-30 noted that this formation offered the advantage that "the platoon leader can keep his platoon under close control as he is able to see all tanks and at the same time search the terrain for targets." The illustration here shows the wedge formation in its most compact form, about 200yd wide and 100yd deep. Recommended formation size could be as great as 400yd and 400yd deep, largely depending on terrain.

The 151st Airborne Tank Company was activated at Fort Knox, Kentucky, on August 15, 1943, followed by the 28th Airborne Tank Battalion on December 6, 1943. These were the only units raised to operate the M22 airborne tank, but neither saw combat service.

> The tank company is normally employed as part of the tank battalion. It may, however, be used as advance, flank, and rear guard and on separate missions. The reinforcement of the tank company will be normal. Such reinforcements will vary from a mortar and an assault gun from the battalion headquarters company to one or more infantry platoons, engineers, artillery, and reconnaissance elements. A light tank company may have a medium tank platoon attached to or supporting it for certain operations.

One difference between the tank company tactics and tank platoon tactics was the greater emphasis placed on the use of terrain:

> The tank is sensitive to terrain. For most efficient use, tanks should operate over terrain that will permit advance by covered routes at good speed. The tank company commander must continually study terrain and seek to turn it to his advantage. The following types should

An M4 medium tank company of the 2d Armored Division takes part in gunnery practice in Britain in late March 1944.

A tank company of the 14th Armored Division adopts a defensive coil position on April 3, 1945, before advancing into Lohr, Germany.

> be avoided: ground covered with large stumps; heavy woods; swamps; ground covered with large boulders; steep slopes. Just because ground appears impassable for tanks does not justify dismissal of possibility of attack either by yourself or the enemy over such ground. Only by detailed reconnaissance can passableness be determined. In many cases passage of difficult ground is justified by surprise effect gained.

Owing to the greater attention paid to the issue of terrain in shaping tank tactics, FM 17-32 also included the first discussion of tank tactics in jungles, an important issue in the PTO:

> In general, because of their sensitiveness to terrain, tanks are unsuited for mass employment in jungles. Their use in such operations will usually be limited to groups of a company or less, supported by infantry. A tank platoon might be attached to an infantry company. Light tanks are more suited to jungle operation than medium tanks. Operation in jungles is usually confined to narrow trails through dense growth relieved at intervals by open spaces. Much of the trail may be swampy and require pioneer work of considerable extent before the tanks can traverse it. [In attacks] Infantry leads on the jungle trails, develops the enemy, and the tanks then attack. Such operations are a continuous series of small attacks; at one time tanks lead and the next, infantry. [In defense] Infantry defends the trails by placing antitank mines and machine guns to cover them. The open spaces are covered by fire. The tanks are held in reserve to counterattack if the enemy succeeds in reaching the open space.

## The armored/tank battalion

Through the summer of 1943, US tank battalions came in two principal varieties: light and medium. Although the M6 heavy tank was accepted for production, the two heavy tank battalions initially planned in 1942 were never created after the production program was canceled.

Initially, there were two configurations of battalions. Those assigned to armored divisions were called armored battalions while those subordinate to the GHQ were called separate tank battalions. The armored battalions

The first separate tank battalion organized by the Armored Force was the 70th Tank Battalion (Light). Co. C is shown here passing for review of President Franklin D. Roosevelt in Morocco during January 1943.

were assigned to the armored regiments of the armored division, with two armored battalions (medium) and one armored battalion (light) per regiment. The separate tank battalions were subordinate to a tank group headquarters, usually on a scale of three battalions per group, with the tank group subordinate to GHQ.

The armored battalion had a headquarters, a headquarters company, and three tank companies. The separate tank battalion was similar in organization to the armored battalion except that a service company was added for administrative purposes and for maintenance. The headquarters and headquarters company consisted of a battalion headquarters and a headquarters company. The battalion headquarters included a tank section with three tanks. The headquarters company was divided into a headquarters section, an assault gun platoon, and a mortar platoon. The company had a small maintenance section for maintenance of company equipment only. FM 17-33 "The Armored Battalion, Light and Medium," released in September 1942, summarized the fundamentals of tank battalion tactics:

An interesting view of an entire tank battalion together in one location. This is the 752d Tank Battalion in front of the Palazzo d'Accursio on Piazza Maggiore shortly after the liberation of Bologna, Italy, on April 21, 1945.

> The tank battalion operates by surprise, fire and maneuver, and concentration of effort (mass). Surprise is obtained by speed of maneuver, use of cover and concealment, striking at an unexpected time in an unexpected direction, and by deceiving the enemy as to the true point of the main attack. Fire and maneuver is a fundamental of all tactical employment. Part of the battalion supports by fire the maneuver of the remainder. This fundamental is applicable down to and including the tank section. Concentration of effort must be made on critical areas. Do not disperse the command by making simultaneous attacks on widely dispersed objectives. Such action is ineffective, wastes effort, and usually leads to failure.
>
> The characteristics of the different type tanks dictate their employment. The light tanks are used to feel out weak points in enemy resistance; to

US armored doctrine discouraged movement in columns in a combat zone because it increased the vulnerability to enemy fire. The exception was movement in column during exploitation against a weakened enemy in order to increase the momentum of an attack. This is a task force of the 4th Armored Division approaching the German city of Erfurt on April 11, 1945.

screen the advance when the situation is vague; as a fast maneuvering force to attack the enemy flank or rear or to exploit a success; to draw the enemy into prepared traps; as advance, flank, or rear guards; on terrain impassable for medium tanks.

The medium tanks are used as the leading wave or echelon of attack against known enemy resistance when the antitank defense is strong; to support by fire the advance of light tanks, other medium tanks, or infantry in tank versus tank action.

## The armored regiment

In contrast to most other armored units, armored regiment tactics underwent fundamental change in 1941–42. The original 1940-pattern armored division included an armored brigade with three armored regiments. The fall 1941 war games led to a substantial redesign and the new March 1942 table of organization and equipment (TO&E) dropped the armored brigade headquarters and reduced the number of armored regiments in the divisions from three to two.

The 1942-pattern armored regiment consisted of a headquarters and headquarters company, a reconnaissance company, a service company, a maintenance company, two armored battalions (medium), and one armored battalion (light). This configuration was short-lived, however. As is described below, the 1943 organization dropped the armored regiment entirely, favoring the use of combat commands to direct the battalions of the armored division. As a result, no field manual for the armored regiment was released during World War II.

The 40th Armored Regiment (Medium), 7th Armored Division, on exercise near Camp Young, California, Desert Training Center, in the spring of 1943. The use of colored flags was common in stateside training, but rare in the combat theaters.

## The armored division

The armored division was the US Army's basic combined-arms formation. Although focused on tanks, it included infantry, artillery, armored cavalry, engineers, and support troops. The configuration of the armored divisions when they made their combat debut in 1942–43 was based on the March 1942 TO&E. This configuration included a headquarters and headquarters company, a service company, an armored signals company, an armored reconnaissance company, two armored regiments, one armored infantry regiment, three armored field artillery battalions, an armored engineer battalion, and divisional trains. The basic tactical guidelines for the armored division were laid out in FM 17-100 "The Armored Division":

> The tactical methods and procedures set forth [in this manual] are not to be considered as inflexible. The employment of the units and weapons of the armored division in many ways and by many methods not described, foreseen, or even contemplated herein, should be sought for and encouraged if such use will be of value in causing the enemy discomfiture and defeat. However, the seeking of such new methods of employment must not interfere with training. Furthermore, any such use must materially contribute to the defeat of the enemy.
>
> The armored division is the basic large armored unit of the combined arms. It comprises troops of the essential arms and services and is organized and equipped as a tactical and administrative self-contained unit capable of independent action to a limited extent. Maintenance, supply, and evacuation units necessary for the conduct of distant operations must be furnished by higher units.
>
> Either by itself or reinforced, the armored division may operate directly under the [field] army. However, it usually operates in a corps consisting of one or more armored divisions and one or more infantry divisions (preferably motorized) or cavalry divisions. The armored division is organized primarily to perform missions that require great mobility and fire power. It is given decisive missions. It is capable of engaging in most forms of combat but *its primary role is in offensive operations against hostile rear areas.*
>
> In general, the role of the infantry division, operating with armored divisions, is to make the opportunity, and the role of the armored division is to exploit it. In performing its role the infantry division secures ground from which the armored division may launch a decisive attack; breaches enemy defenses so the armored division may pass through the gap created and exploit the success; or forms a base of maneuver for the armored division. The armored division exploits the success of the infantry by launching an attack to destroy

An M4 medium tank of the 4th Armored Division moves past a light machine gun position of one of the division's armored infantry battalions on January 3, 1945, outside Bastogne, France, a week after the division had made its legendary race from the Sarr region to relieve Bastogne.

enemy installations or formations, and to seize critical terrain.

The armored division should be free to take advantage of its mobility to defeat the enemy decisively. Mobile infantry should follow closely behind the armored division to protect the flanks and the rear, relieve the armored infantry, protect reorganization, free the armored division for further action, and provide security for the armored division during darkness.

The tank commander of "Duration III," an M4A3(76mm) of the 11th Armored Division, scrutinizes the village of Kappel, Austria, on May 4, 1945, while two accompanying armored infantrymen take shots at outlying buildings.

Combined-arms tactics in armored divisions were substantially different from separate tank battalions supporting infantry divisions. The armored infantry battalions were an organic element of the divisions, and the tank and armored infantry battalions regularly trained and operated together. Armored infantry battalions transported their troops by armored halftrack. The armored infantry remained in the halftracks as far forward as possible to conserve their energy, to speed the advance, to reduce casualties in crossing areas swept by small-arms fire and fragments, and to use the firepower of machine guns on the halftracks. Combined tank/armored infantry tactics fell roughly into two categories, mounted and dismounted actions, and were dependent both on terrain and the intensity of enemy opposition.

Tank/armored infantry actions could involve a battalion of each type in a combat command, or varying mixtures of tank and armored infantry companies in a task force. Dismounted actions were by far the most common tactics because they allowed the infantry to seize and mop up the objective and to complete the destruction of the enemy. Even after the majority of the riflemen dismounted, halftracks still had troops on board to man the vehicle machine guns to give close support to the dismounted personnel. The tank/infantry tactics varied depending on the objective and there were numerous options. The most common tactical options were:

- Tanks provided supporting fire then joined dismounted infantry in the assault.
- Tanks and dismounted armored infantry approached the objective from different directions.
- Tanks supported dismounted armored infantry by overhead or flanking fire.
- Armored infantrymen rode the tanks to the objective.
- Tanks and dismounted armored infantry advanced together.
- Tanks initially provided supporting fire then passed through the dismounted armored infantry and preceded them to the objective.

Mounted actions were most common during exploitation missions on which speed was essential and enemy resistance light. There were three principal tactical approaches to mounted actions: a mixed formation of tanks and halftracks; halftracks following the tanks by short successive bounds; and tanks and armored infantry converging on the objective from different directions.

# US TANK TACTICS MATURE: 1943

In 1943, the US Army's tank units underwent their most extensive organizational and tactical changes as a result of combat lessons from the fighting in Tunisia, Sicily, and the Italian mainland. These actions were the first combat uses of US Army armored divisions and highlighted the need for many significant improvements.

## Operations in North Africa and Sicily

In November 1942, elements of the US Army's 1st and 2d Armored Divisions and 70th Tank Battalion (Light) took part in the Operation *Torch* landings in French North Africa. The 2d Armored Division remained in French North Africa as a shield against a potential German strike via Spain. In the meantime, the US Army's II Corps, including the 1st Armored Division and the 1st and 34th Infantry divisions, headed for Tunisia to confront the 5. Panzerarmee as part of the multinational forces under the British First Army.

The defeat of the 1st Armored Division during the fighting for Kasserine Pass in February 1943 raised serious questions about US preparedness, tactical doctrine, and organization. To its credit, the US Army undertook extensive investigations into the shortcomings, leading to numerous internal reports. Special observers were sent to North Africa, and delegations of high-ranking US Army leaders visited the battlefields to investigate personally. Among those on fact-finding missions were Major General Jacob L. Devers, commander of the Armored Force from August 1941 to May 1943, and his successor, Major General Alvan C. Gillem, Jr. An assessment by Combat Command B, 1st Armored Division, in June 1943 concluded that:

> Generally speaking, the tactical doctrine as laid down in our field manuals has proven to be sound. The weakness lies in the fact that during the high tempo of battle, and more especially with green and untried commands, a great many times elementary military teaching

One of the most influential officers in the creation of the Armored Force was Major General Jacob L. Devers, shown here on September 3, 1941, in front of the T6 pilot for the M4A1 medium tank. He was commander of the Armored Force from August 1941 to May 1943 before assuming command of the US Army in Europe prior to Eisenhower's appointment.

is forgotten or overlooked with the result that unnecessary lives are lost and often times the tide of battle runs with disastrous results.

In October 1943, the War Department published a small booklet entitled "Training Lessons from the Tunisian Campaign" that attempted to summarize the key lessons learned. Regarding armored units, the report concluded that:

The crew of an M3 medium tank of Co. D, 2/13th Armored, 1st Armored Division, load 75mm ammunition near Souk El Arbaa, Tunisia, on November 23, 1942. This was the last battalion of the division still equipped with the M3 medium tank.

> The outstanding general lesson of the campaign was failure to use the [1st] Armored Division in sufficient strength or in concentrated mass. The [1st Armored Division] was not employed as a unit until the final phases of the battles for Mateur and Bizerte. Previous to these actions, the armor "arrived piecemeal and was piecemeal throughout" ... Offensive action by American [armored] troops was marked by a dispersal of effort. Mass action was in fact precluded by the necessity of spreading the [1st Armored Division] over a wide front because it was the only force available with sufficient mobility and power to meet sudden [German] thrusts over a long and thin line. The above-mentioned employment, though justified by necessity, should be recognized as contrary to established doctrine.

Two particular engagements stood out as examples of inexperience, rash command decisions, and failure to follow basic tactical doctrine. On February 14, 1943, two companies of the 3d Battalion, 1st Armored Regiment, stumbled into the advancing 10. Panzer-Division near Djebel Lessouda and were wiped out. The following day, the 2d Battalion, 1st Armored Regiment, was wiped out when it rushed headlong into a German Panzer ambush near Sidi bou Zid. Examination of these engagements led to the following remarks in the Tunisia booklet:

> Another lesson from the campaign stems from the inaccurate picture of speed and aggressiveness that had been common in the United States with regard to armored action. Units must not charge blindly into action with the reckless audacity associated with the overworked phrase "Blitzkrieg." On the contrary, they must work forward steadily, skillfully, and with determination, utilizing every means of reconnaissance and covering fire at the disposal of the command.

Although senior commanders were convinced of the basic soundness of US Army tank tactics, lower-ranking officers were critical of the unrealistic solutions offered in field manuals and training when dealing with common

A pair of M4 medium tanks of Co. F, 1st Armored Regiment, 1st Armored Division, knocked out by German tank-gun fire on February 15, 1943, near Sidi Salem during the Kasserine Pass battle. Inexperience and failed tactics led to heavy casualties among the green US Army tank troops in Tunisia.

battlefield problems. One report from the 1st Armored Division gave an example from the theoretical textbook solutions to dealing with enemy antitank guns that led to overconfidence on the part of US Army tank crews in dealing with the threat:

> In the Armored Force Field manuals, one obtains the idea from scanning the cleverly designed sketches of "do's and don'ts" of small unit operations that it is desirable and proper for armor to attack anti-tank gun positions. Many sketches show varied methods of approach toward subduing anti-tank guns. Experience has proven, at least in the Tunisian campaign, that the anti-tank gun is to be avoided as much as possible and only attacked as a last resort. While the sketches are for the most part correct in methods to be used, still it should be more strongly emphasized that anti-tank positions should be avoided by tanks and only attacked when no other means of overcoming them is available ... [the manuals] created a false picture and also a feeling of overconfidence. In the initial stages of the operation by [CCB, 1st Armored Division] in November–December 1942, such overconfidence resulted in the rapid whittling down of a medium tank battalion to less than twenty tanks within a few minutes of actual combat.

The next major campaign after Tunisia was Operation *Husky*, the amphibious landings on Sicily in July 1943. The Seventh US Army under Lieutenant General George S. Patton, Jr., deployed the veteran 2d Armored Division and 70th Tank Battalion (Light) on Sicily. In contrast to the fighting in Tunisia, Patton employed the 2d Armored Division in textbook fashion, using it in a race from the southern Sicilian coast to the key port of Palermo. Although there was study of the "Lessons Learned" in Tunisia, the improved performance of US armored units led to fewer suggestions for tactical remedies.

## Lessons learned

The most significant organizational change resulting from the experiences in Tunisia and Sicily was the configuration of the armored division. Even after the reorganization of the armored divisions in March 1942, they were still too tank-heavy and too weak in supporting arms. During the North African fighting, it was frequently necessary to attach units from neighboring infantry divisions to the armored division combat commands, especially during defensive operations. As a result, Lieutenant General Lesley J. McNair, commander of the Army Ground Forces (AGF), authorized a shift in the mix of tank/infantry/artillery battalions in the armored division from the March 1942 ratio of 6:3:3 ratio to 3:3:3. The armored regiment organization was abandoned, and in its place the three component tank battalions remained. In place of the armored regiment headquarters, the new organization marked a final shift to the combat command method of organization with the division's nine combat battalions parceled out to the three combat commands, now designated as CCA, CCB, and CCR (reserve). The newer configuration was an effort to accentuate the combined-arms orientation of the division and away from its original tank focus.

The armored division change took place in September 1943 and was not without controversy. Lieutenant General Devers, after commanding the Armored Force, had been appointed in May 1943 to head the European Theater of Operations United States Army (ETOUSA), and felt that the reorganization was unwise for the 2d and 3d Armored Divisions that were already deployed in England in late 1943. As a result, these two divisions retained the so-called "heavy" 1942 configuration although with some modifications such as the adoption of the new mixed tank battalion organization. The 1st Armored Division, rebuilding in North Africa after its losses in the earlier Tunisian campaign, was earmarked for deployment to Italy over the next few months. Rather than subject it to more turmoil, McNair and the AGF agreed to let it remain in the 1942 "heavy" configuration until its next major refit that did not occur until July 1944 after the Anzio operation and the capture of Rome.

The fighting in Tunisia made it clear that the day of the light tank had passed. The 37mm gun on the M3 and M5 light tanks was inadequate and the tanks' armor was too thin since the advent of the German 50mm and 75mm antitank guns. Owing to the failure of the M7 light tank program, many US Army tank officers wanted to retire the light tank outright. In September 1943, however, the US Army still had 3,045 light tanks and 4,575 medium tanks in the continental United States, so declaring 40 percent of the US Army tank fleet obsolete was deemed too extreme. The AGF decided on a compromise. The distinction between light tank and medium tank battalions was abolished, and a new standard battalion TO&E was adopted. This new standard tank battalion had three companies of M4 medium tanks and one company of M5A1 light tanks. The light tanks were intended to perform secondary missions such as reconnaissance, flank security and other roles tailored to their limitations.

For reasons that remain obscure, a handful of battalions remained configured as light tank battalions. These were very rare, with only a single example, the 758th in the MTO in 1944–45, and only two, the 744th and 759th Tank Battalions (Light), in the ETO.

The other significant development in the wake of the fighting in Tunisia was the role of the separate tank battalions. The idea of using three tank battalions under an armored group command as a mini-armored division had not proven practical. In Tunisia, the 751st Tank Battalion (Medium) had been assigned to support the 34th Infantry Division. This had proven to be a successful team, and there was a widespread recognition that infantry divisions needed continual tank support in battle. Lieutenant General Devers specifically noted that more attention had to be paid to the orphaned separate tank battalions. A reorientation of their tactical doctrine back to the prewar infantry support role was warranted because the existing doctrine was poorly defined and nearly useless in combat.

This revival of interest in infantry/tank cooperation coincided with the reorganization of the US Army's armored divisions. Under the March 1942 TO&E, each division had six tank battalions but under the new 1943 TO&E, they were reduced to three tank battalions. Suddenly, more than 40 tank battalions that had been organic to the armored divisions were now free for a new role. Clearly, more attention had to be paid to the tactics of this large force.

As early as March 1943, the AGF operations officer, Brigadier General John M. Lentz, argued that the separate tank battalions were a bad idea and that the tank units should be made organic to the infantry divisions. His boss, Lieutenant General McNair, opposed this idea, as he still favored his modular infantry division concept. McNair also felt that separate battalions could provide a vital mass of firepower and maneuver in the forthcoming campaign in France. Instead of formal incorporation of tank battalions into the infantry divisions, McNair issued a directive in April 1943 stressing the need for more combined training by tank and infantry units.

In spite of this order, tank battalions were still too few in number to permit each infantry division to train with a tank battalion. Furthermore, the tank battalions and infantry divisions were seldom located together at the same base. In June 1943, Major General Walton H. Walker, commanding general of IV Corps, returning from Tunisia, suggested a more practical solution – that separate tank battalions after receiving basic unit training, be stationed with a corresponding infantry division for further training, and remain with that division during entry into combat. When the new commander of the Armored Command, Lieutenant General Gillem, returned from his fact-finding mission to Sicily in July 1943, he also tried to reinvigorate the tank/infantry issue. In spite of McNair's opposition, there was gathering

**LEFT**
Patton's employment of the 2d Armored Division on Sicily reflected a better understanding of US tactical doctrine. Here, a column of M4A1 medium tanks enters Palermo on July 22, 1943, after a race across western Sicily to the northern coast.

**RIGHT**
One of the more outlandish schemes to foster tank/infantry cooperation was the infantry sled, shown here being demonstrated near Cisterna, Italy, in May 1944. The brainchild of Major General John W. O'Daniel, commander of the 3d Infantry Division, a dozen sleds were towed by a single medium tank of the 756th Tank Battalion. Although used during the Anzio breakout, the concept was detested by the infantry.

Terrain restrictions in Italy left tank battalions idle. In many cases, they were used instead to deepen divisional artillery in the indirect-fire role, as shown here with M4 medium tanks of the 755th Tank Battalion near Pietramala, Italy, on October 1, 1944.

momentum to abandon the mission of the massed use of separate tank battalions to support the corps or army, to the dedicated use of the tank battalions to provide direct support to infantry divisions.

These debates indicated that the pendulum had swung back again to the traditional role of separate tank battalions. The tactical doctrine of US Army tank battalions from 1918 to 1940 had been the support of the infantry; but the shocking defeat of France in 1940 had led to a fundamental shift in the mission of the tank force, at the expense of its traditional role. By late 1943, the US Army had come to recognize that the two missions were not mutually exclusive. The armored divisions could be used as the US Army's main striking force, while at the same time, a significant fraction of the tank force would be used in the less dramatic, but equally important, mission of supporting the infantry.

The main problem in implementing this tactical change was the lack of time. By the fall of 1943, the US Army was in considerable turmoil as units were being transferred from stateside training to combat assignments in Europe and the Pacific. As a result, tank battalions received little or no significant training with infantry units stateside prior to the summer of 1944. There were also problems in conducting joint exercises in Britain in the spring of 1944 due to the congestion of all the US units being funneled into the UK for the invasion. What training that did occur was often unrealistic. The US Army in 1943–44 did not have a great deal of practical experience in fighting of the type that would be encountered in Europe in 1944–45. Lessons from the Italian campaign were slow in making their way through the system and were not entirely applicable to the situations that would arise in France.

The revived focus on tank/infantry cooperation was not only a problem in the separate tank battalions. Just as importantly, senior infantry commanders were unprepared to employ tank units properly in conjunction with infantry divisions. There was no established doctrine until the publication of FM 17-36 "Armored Employment of Tanks with Infantry," in March 1944. Although this field manual was made available prior to the D-Day landings in Normandy in June 1944, there was little time for these guidelines to filter down to the tank and infantry units. Furthermore, the doctrine was not entirely mature, with some substantial gaps such as the lack of a practical radio-net between the infantry and supporting tank units. These issues would have to be developed in the heat of combat in Normandy and the Pacific.

# TANK TACTICS IN COMBAT 1944–45

## Tank tactics in ETO amphibious landings

The first mission of the US armored force in the ETO was the support of the infantry landings in Normandy on June 6, 1944. US amphibious landing tactics had evolved considerably from their debut in November 1942 during Operation *Torch*. The US Army had developed a waterproofing system called a deep-wading kit that allowed a tank to be driven off a landing craft in shallow water and drive up the beach without flooding its engine or electrical system. This was first used during Operation *Torch*, mainly on M5 light tanks. The main problem in 1942 was the shortage of dedicated tank landing vessels such as the Landing Craft Tank (LCT) and Landing Ship Tank (LST). These became more widely available for Operation *Husky* on Sicily in July 1943 and again were used in conjunction with deep-wading tanks.

The British Army had different amphibious experiences than the US Army, notably the heavy losses suffered by LCTs at the August 1942 landings at Dieppe. This led to the development of a new method of landing tanks, the Duplex Drive or DD tank. These tanks were fitted with a canvas enclosure to increase their buoyancy to permit them to "swim" ashore, allowing the LCTs to remain safe offshore. The Normandy landings were largely prepared by a British staff that favored the DD tank approach for the initial waves of tanks in Operation *Neptune* in Normandy. By the time that US staff became involved, these decisions had largely been made. Lieutenant General Devers and the ETOUSA were badgered into the use of DD tanks for the landings.

The commander of the US V Corps, Major General Leonard T. Gerow, was opposed to the use of DD tanks due to their fragility when swimming. In his view, the solution to the Dieppe problem was tactical not technical – do not land at a heavily defended port like Dieppe. That was the premise of Operation *Neptune* because Lower Normandy was selected specifically for the perceived weakness of the German defenses. By the time Gerow took

The first use of the Project "Blue Freeze" deep-wading kits for amphibious landings was Operation *Torch* in November 1942. This is a group of M5 light tanks of Co. C, 756th Tank Battalion, on Pier 4 at Newport News, Virginia, on October 20, 1942, part of Task Force A with the transport ship USS *Lyons* (AP-71) in the background, prior to their departure for North Africa.

The M4A1 medium tank in the foreground with deep-wading trunks was the dozer tank of Lieutenant Frank A. Klotz, leader of the dozer platoon of the 741st Tank Battalion in the Coleville sur-Mer sector of Omaha Beach, supporting the initial assault wave of the 16th Infantry, 1st Infantry Division. This tank lost its blade on D-Day. The tank behind is from Co. A.

command of V Corps for the Omaha Beach landings, the DD production program in the US was already underway. Instead, a compromise was reached. The three US Army tank battalions landing in the first waves in Normandy would have an expedient organization of two companies of DD tanks and one company of deep-wading tanks; follow-on battalions would have all deep-wading tanks.

Navy and Army officers tried to work around the vulnerability of the DD tanks by implementing guidelines in the event of heavy seas, with instructions to land the DD tanks directly on shore from their LCTs in the event of heavy waves. These informal understandings fell victim to the fog of war. On the eastern side of Omaha Beach, the Army captains leading the two DD companies of the 741st Tank Battalion decided to try to swim ashore in spite of the heavy waves, and all but five of their tanks sank. On the western side of Omaha Beach, the Navy officer in charge recognized the hazard of the wave conditions on D-Day morning and landed the 743d Tank Battalion directly on shore from the LCTs under his command with far better results. On Utah Beach, the battle-hardened 70th Tank Battalion benefited from far less dangerous sea conditions and landed their tanks with far less chaos than on Omaha Beach.

The tanks on Omaha Beach played an essential role in the early hours of the landing, knocking out several of the most dangerous German strongpoints. The unique topography of Omaha Beach, with its high bluffs and few access roads, was better suited to the German defense preparations than the other Operation *Neptune* beaches. By blocking the exits from the beach with reinforced strongpoints, and creating minefields on the bluffs, the Germans trapped the first waves of US Army troops in an exceptionally dangerous killing zone on the beach. The terrain confined the surviving tanks on Omaha Beach with little room to maneuver during the remainder of D-Day. One US infantry commander later remarked that the tanks had "saved the day. They shot the hell out of the Germans and got the hell shot out of them."

The situation on Utah Beach was significantly different because the terrain posed little barrier to the tanks exiting the beach. The German defenses there were far less fearsome than on Omaha Beach. As a result, the 70th Tank Battalion was able to carry out its mission of supporting the 4th Infantry Division in pushing out of the beachhead into the countryside beyond.

Although DD tanks had very mixed results during the Operation *Neptune* landings in Normandy, they were more successful in the Operation *Dragoon* landings in southern France on August 15, 1944. Here, riflemen of the 15th Infantry, 3d Infantry Division, are on Alpha Yellow beach near Saint-Tropez with a DD tank of the 756th Tank Battalion behind them.

The DD tanks were used again during Operation *Dragoon*, the US landings on the Mediterranean coast of France on August 15, 1944. In this case, the water conditions were relatively calm, and the DD tanks swam ashore with little difficulty. There was another attempt to use them in March 1945 for the Rhine River crossings, but by this time, the technical condition of their swimming skirts was so poor that most US DD tanks were driven over bridges rather than swimming the Rhine. DD tanks were not used in the PTO, with both the US Army and US Marine Corps relying on deep-wading tactics starting with the Kwajalein landings in February 1944.

## Tank/infantry cooperation: separate tank battalions

In June 1944 after D-Day, the First US Army began stuffing more and more armored units into the Normandy beachhead. This included separate tank battalions as well as the 2d and 3d Armored Divisions. In keeping with US tactical doctrine, the 2d and 3d Armored Divisions were kept in reserve until the infantry divisions could provide an opportunity for their use. Although there were a few small-scale uses of task forces from the armored divisions, they were not used en masse until Operation *Cobra* in late July 1944. As a result, separate tank battalions bore the brunt of the US tank fighting in Normandy for the first six weeks of the campaign.

US tank combat in the Normandy beachhead area was conducted in the face of several serious tactical problems. As mentioned earlier, the tactics of the separate tank battalions in infantry support were still in flux because the US Army had not issued clear tactical guidelines until March 1944 and many units had not received the new field manuals nor trained using these tactics. There had been minimal cross-training between separate tank battalions and infantry divisions in Britain before D-Day. As a result, tactics had to be improvised. To their credit, tank battalions and infantry divisions quickly adapted to the circumstances. A lingering technical problem plagued tank/infantry cooperation, however: the incompatibility of tank and infantry radios. Finally, tank/infantry tactics were constrained by the local French terrain in the Calvados region of Lower Normandy, called *bocage*.

**LEFT**
Tank/infantry cooperation in armored divisions was simplified because the armored infantry battalions were organic to the division and regularly operated alongside tank battalions. Here a squad from Co. C, 61st Armored Infantry Battalion, CCA, 10th Armored Division, dismounts during fighting near Bubenorbis, Germany, on April 17, 1945.

**RIGHT**
On March 7, 1945, the 76th Infantry Division assaulted and captured the town of Binsfeld, Germany, supported by tanks of the 702d Tank Battalion. This is a view of one of its companies outside the town with an M4A1 in the immediate foreground and an M32 tank recovery vehicle to the left.

Tanks provided the infantry with a vital asset to overcome entrenched German defenses and machine-gun nests. Infantry was vital to tanks in close terrain because the tanks were virtually blind while the infantry could quickly detect threats such as emplaced antitank guns and German infantry equipped with *Panzerfaust* antitank rocket launchers. Tanks could help capture objectives while infantry was essential to holding objectives once they were seized.

A typical mission in Normandy illustrates the problem. On June 9, the 747th Tank Battalion was supporting the 175th Infantry, 29th Infantry Division, in an attempt to capture Isigny-sur-Mer near Omaha Beach. At 0300hrs, the tanks pushed into Isigny, but the infantry did not follow. Heavy fire against the tanks from troops of the 352. Infanterie-Division and the threat of German antitank weapons such as the *Panzerfaust* convinced the tankers to withdraw from the town. The town was captured later in the day after the 175th Infantry Regiment repulsed a German counterattack. The 29th Infantry Division and 747th Tank Battalion remained in operation together until withdrawn on June 21 for their first joint training in tank/infantry cooperation to overcome the local *bocage* terrain.

The frequent lack of cross-training between tank and infantry units before combat created a lack of confidence between both combat arms. A report by a tank battalion in the Pacific holds true for this problem, even if in a different theater:

> A direct result of this lack of training was a feeling of distrust between the [infantry and armor]. It evolved from a misunderstanding of each other's capabilities and limitations. Infantry commanders felt that the tanks were not sufficiently aggressive when they wouldn't push blindly out in the face of the enemy who had stopped the foot soldiers. In return, the tanker felt that when the going got stiff and the lead started flying, the infantryman would desert him. If the tanker couldn't see the accompanying infantry, he immediately surmised that he had been abandoned not realizing that in the close underbrush, the infantryman was still there but had merely crouched down to avoid being a larger target. This situation was further aggravated by the lack of tank-infantry communications and the whole business became a major problem when the weather, heat, and mud increased. It finally

straightened itself out as the tankers and infantrymen became used to each other and learned expensively to be sure just what each could, would, and was prepared to do in support of each other. By the end of the campaign, the tank-infantry team was pretty well coordinated and bound together by mutual trust and respect.

The problems of tank/infantry cooperation were addressed by the armored group headquarters. These brigade headquarters were originally created to exercise tactical command over three tank battalions on independent missions. This role largely disappeared in 1944 due to the trend to attach separate tank battalions to infantry divisions for direct support. Instead, the armored groups were mainly used for administrative purposes and were used as an impromptu armored section in corps headquarters to advise the corps about tank issues including tactics, availability, and supply. So, for example, the 3d Armored Group was subordinate to V Corps from D-Day and beyond. In early June, it managed five separate tank battalions: 741st, 743d, 745th, 747th, and 759th (Light). The usual practice was to allot one separate tank battalion per infantry division. In general, one tank company would be attached to each of the division's three infantry regiments. The armored group headquarters became the main advocates for greater training between tank battalions and infantry divisions before both were committed to action. If this was not possible, the armored group headquarters usually fostered meetings between tank battalion officers and their associated infantry officers to work out details of forthcoming combat missions.

Tank/infantry cooperation was worked out through combat experience. During the 1944–45 fighting in the ETO, the US Army found that separate tank battalions suffered about half of their wartime losses in the first 4–6 weeks of combat. No matter how good the training, actual combat was necessary for tank battalions to become acclimated to the battlefield.

The tactical problems identified in Normandy can be discerned from operations reports of the infantry divisions. One of the best of these was issued by the 1st Infantry Division following their experiences with the 745th Tank Battalion in Normandy. This excellent tactics memorandum was subsequently circulated by AGF to all divisions and headquarters in September 1944:

The essential duo in armored divisions was the tank and armored infantry halftrack. Here an M3A1 halftrack passes by an M4A3(76mm) medium tank of Co. B, 48th Tank Battalion, 14th Armored Division, knocked out during the bloody fighting for Barr in the Alsace region of France on November 28, 1944.

The following principles are basic and should never be disregarded. (a) Tanks must not be employed individually. The movement of every tank in a combat zone should be covered by fire of another tank. In order best to implement this principle, tanks should be employed by platoons (5 tanks). (b) The liaison between tanks and accompanying infantry must be close and continuous. In close-country the infantry should precede the tanks and screen their flanks. In more open country, and in the absence of enemy anti-tank defenses, tanks may precede, but must never outrun, the infantry

**LEFT**
Soldiers of the 23d Armored Infantry Battalion supporting an M4A3(76mm) of the 7th Armored Division near Hünningen (Hunnange), Belgium, on January 23, 1945, at the end of the Ardennes campaign.

**RIGHT**
Troops of the 55th Armored Infantry Battalion advance ahead of an M4A3(76mm) of the 22d Tank Battalion, 11th Armored Division, during fighting in Wernberg, Germany, on April 22, 1945.

or get beyond the reach of infantry supporting fires. (c) Tanks must never be emplaced, or left standing, in a position where they are under enemy observation or are likely to be discovered and surprised by enemy patrols by day or by night. (d) Routes of advance for tanks under fire must be reconnoitered in advance by tank personnel, so far as possible. Routes will be reconnoitered and tanks will be guided by infantry personnel especially assigned to this task when the advance goes beyond the limits of the reconnaissance which the tank crews have been able to make. (e) Tanks must be given assistance by ground troops in the breaching and in the detection of minefields. (f) Tanks must not be expected to attack enemy anti-tank guns frontally or unassisted by infantry fires and artillery. (g) Tank–infantry joint operations raise problems of liaison, communications, control, and mutual confidence. Such operations will not be successful unless the attachment of tanks to the infantry units with which they are to fight is made in sufficient time to allow the tank crews and infantrymen to arrive at solutions to their joint liaison and tactical problems and to develop a degree of mutual understanding and confidence. (h) Provisions must be made for refueling, re-arming, and giving first echelon maintenance to tanks during the course of any extended action in which they are involved. Further provision must be made to relieve the tanks for a return to the rear in order to carry out required higher echelon maintenance checks or for the accomplishment of repairs shown to be necessary by first echelon checks where such repairs cannot be made in the forward area.

## The technical dilemma: tank/infantry radio communication

Aside from basic tactical principles, a lingering problem was the lack of a practical means of tank/infantry communication at platoon and company level. This was critical because the lack of an easy means of communication made tank/infantry cooperation at the small-unit level very difficult. This was primarily an issue in separate tank battalions attached to infantry divisions because the armored divisions were equipped with radios that permitted coordination between the tanks and infantry halftracks.

The infantry used the handheld SCR-586 "handie-talkie" at the platoon level. This was an AM radio transceiver, but the standard tank radios such

**LEFT**
This inconspicuous box was a major innovation in tank/infantry tactics when adopted in the summer of 1944. It consists of an EE-8 field telephone wired into the tank's intercom system to permit accompanying riflemen to speak directly to the tank crew. It was stowed in an empty .30-caliber machine-gun ammunition box.

**RIGHT**
For close air support missions, a tank in the task force was fitted with specialized ground–air radios operated by select fighter pilots. During an operation along the Siegfried Line in the fall of 1944, Lieutenant Charles R. Earls of the 395th Fighter Squadron enters the turret of an M4 medium tank while Brigadier General Truman E. Boudinot, commander of CCB, 3d Armored Division, looks on.

as the SCR-508 were FM transceivers, so they could not talk to one another. A new FM infantry radio, the backpack SCR-300 "walkie-talkie" was being introduced into infantry companies in the summer of 1944, but this was in short supply; and although it operated in the FM mode, it transmitted in different frequency bands than the tank FM radios and so did not solve the communication problems.

The existing textbook solution for tank/infantry communication was too time-consuming and cumbersome. For example, an infantry section spotted a German antitank gun hiding in a hedge that was aimed at a supporting M4 tank. The infantry wanted to warn the M4's crew. The textbook process required the platoon leader to start the message process via the platoon's SCR-586 to a company SCR-586, then to the company FM SCR-300, to the infantry battalion headquarters' FM SCR-294, and then down the tank battalion chain of command from the FM SCR-506 of the tank battalion HQ to the supporting tank company HQ and then to the individual tank's FM radio. The German antitank gun would have fired long before the communication network routed the radio call from the infantry platoon to the tank.

The earliest solution to this problem was to give an EE-8 field telephone to the forward tank and then run telephone wire behind the tank to accompanying infantry. This could work, but once the tank began the move, there was a high probability that the telephone wire would be broken. Nevertheless, this technique was widely used in Normandy despite its obvious shortcomings.

**C**

**TANK/INFANTRY COOPERATION: TECHNICAL INNOVATIONS**
The addition of a field telephone connection at the rear of the tank in the summer of 1944 was a major technical improvement in tank/infantry cooperation. This consisted of an EE-8 field telephone connected to the tank's RC-99 Interphone Equipment. The initial conversions were locally wired in Normandy, but the Signal Corps developed the RC-298 Interphone Extension Kit to standardize and facilitate the process. The telephone was initially mounted in a .30-caliber machine-gun ammunition box, but later in the war, a dedicated armored box was issued for this process. This system enabled a soldier behind the tank to communicate directly to the crew inside. The kit eventually included a buzzer that would alert the tank crew that that a soldier wished to speak to them, prompting them to switch on the interphone connection.

The other obvious solution was to provide one of the tanks with an infantry radio such as an SCR-586 handie-talkie or the larger SCR-300. The first problem with this was that the tank hatch had to be left open for the antenna to protrude, and the tankers were not keen on that risk in close terrain. The second problem was that a moving tank generated strong radio frequency interference which could overlap the frequencies used by the AM radios, essentially creating "noise" that disrupted the radio signal. This was the reason that US tanks used FM radios that could suppress this interference. Finally, these infantry radios were in perennially short supply in Normandy.

In June 1944, an unrecorded soldier, reportedly from the 743d Tank Battalion, came up with the idea of connecting an EE-8 field telephone into the tank's intercom system. This removed the need for a trailing wire, though it did require an infantryman to follow closely behind the tank. This system had many foibles, however, not the least of which was faulty wiring that short-circuited the tank's intercom system, much to the chagrin of the tank crew. The armored group headquarters were informed of this innovation and the First US Army set about a more formal process for equipping tanks with tank/infantry telephones. A proper wiring arrangement was developed, and the telephones were mounted in .30-caliber machine-gun ammunition boxes at the rear corner of the tank to provide protection. In anticipation of Operation *Cobra* in late July, a program was underway to equip all tanks in separate tank battalions with this feature. It is interesting to note that an identical process was underway in the Pacific with much the same results. The first extensive use of tank/infantry telephones by US Army and US Marine Corps tank battalions took place in July 1944 on Saipan and Guam.

The longer-term solution was the AN/VRC-3 FM radio, a tank-mounted version of the infantry's SCR-300 that operated in the same frequency bands. The new June 1944 tank battalion TO&E change authorized one AN/VRC-3 for each tank company HQ and two per tank platoon. These began arriving in September 1944 and were gradually introduced into the tank battalions by December. In combination with the tank-mounted field telephone, this helped overcome the problems with tank/infantry communication.

## *Bocage*-busting tactics

The terrain in the Calvados region of Lower Normandy posed a significant tactical problem to the First US Army in June–July 1944. Locally called *bocage*, the network of hedgerows created a difficult terrain obstacle. From a military perspective, the hedgerows created a network of inverted trenches, forming a natural, layered fortification system that was well suited to defense. The earthen base of the hedgerow shielded the German defenders from small-arms and machine-gun fire. The vegetation on top of the hedgerow provided concealment for the defenders and restricted the observation of the attacking force. In addition, the hedgerows provided a solid basis for foxholes to shield against mortar and artillery fire. The *bocage* severely constrained maneuver by the US infantry, and even more so for tanks. A US after-action report noted that: "The supporting tanks suffered unduly high casualties in attempting to do this…Germans concealed in the hedgerows and employing antitank guns, rocket launchers, and antitank grenades took a heavy toll among the tanks, especially when the [tanks] had attempted to climb the hedgerows." The Wehrmacht expertly adapted this terrain to create a formidable defense. The *bocage* constrained the use of tanks to assist

**LEFT**
The initial style of hedgerow cutters such as the "Salad Fork" shown here were too fragile. As can be seen on this example of an M4 of the 747th Tank Battalion, the two pointed timbers on the bow have been smashed upward after impact with the hedgerow.

**RIGHT**
An M4A1(76mm) of the 2d Armored Division crunches through *bocage* with a Culin Rhino device during the opening phases of Operation *Cobra* in July 1944.

the infantry until the development of tactics and devices that permitted the tanks to penetrate and overcome the hedgerows.

The most obvious technical solution was to use a tank-dozer to bulldoze a break into the hedgerows. The main problem was the shortage of dozer tanks. These had entered production in April 1944 and only about three-dozen were available to the First US Army in Normandy. Because obstacle breaching is a traditional engineer task, US Army engineer units began to explore possible techniques for penetrating the hedgerows. One method was explosive breaching. In late June 1944, the 2d Infantry Division set up a rear-area school to examine hedgerow fighting tactics. The new tactics centered on a combined-arms team:

> This team consisted of one rifle squad, one engineer demolition detachment of four men, and one medium tank. The function of the engineers was to clear a path for the tank through the hedgerows. They accomplished this by placing two satchel charges on the hedgerow and igniting them. Each satchel charge consisted of twenty pounds of TNT and eleven such charges were carried on each tank. The explosion caused by a pair of these charges placed on a hedgerow would blow a gap through which a tank could cross without exposing its belly to hostile fire.

This new tactic was first used during the attack on Hill 192 on July 11, 1944. In the meantime, the 121st Engineer Combat Battalion of the 29th Infantry Division had also been conducting *bocage*-breaching experiments in late June 1944 along with the division's attached tank unit, the 747th Tank Battalion. This was a modified version of the 2d Division technique, with the M4s fitted with a "Salad Fork" of two sharpened logs on their bow to quickly create tunnels at the base of the hedgerow. This significantly sped up the process of explosively breaching the hedgerow. The new tactics were used during the July 11 attack by the 116th Infantry Regiment and accompanying tanks. The new tactics and devices helped the 116th Infantry Regiment rupture the German defenses far more effectively than in the past.

The main problem with explosive breaching was the volume of explosives required. A tank company penetrating 1½ miles through *bocage* country would encounter 34 separate hedgerows. This would require 17 tons of explosive per company or about 60 tons per battalion – clearly beyond the resources of any engineer battalion.

An M4 of the 746th Tank Battalion fitted with a Rhino hedgerow cutter escorts riflemen of Co. I, 60th Infantry, 9th Infantry Division, during fighting near the Belgian border on September 9, 1944.

During the training, the 747th Tank Battalion discovered that the Salad Fork alone could not penetrate the hedgerow. The main problem was that the log prongs were easily snapped off. As a result, the battalion began experimenting with steel prongs. News of this development was spread through the other tank battalions in Normandy via the network of armored group headquarters. The best known of the resulting hedgerow cutters was the Rhino, designed by Sergeant Curtis G. Culin, Jr., of the 102d Cavalry Reconnaissance Squadron. This was demonstrated to the V Corps commander, Major General Gerow, and subsequently to the First US Army commander, Lieutenant General Bradley, on July 14. Bradley saw the Rhino as an important technical solution to the tactical problem of the *bocage* and ordered the mass-production of the device in time for the forthcoming Operation *Cobra* offensive. Although Culin's Rhino was the most famous of these devices, other designs were developed and built by other units.

The use of the hedgerow cutters during Operation *Cobra* had mixed results. As is described below, the armored divisions preferred to exploit the speed potential of the available road network rather than grind through the *bocage*. Separate tank battalions confronting the hedgerows found the cutters useful, however, as noted in this after-action report:

> The attack was launched as planned at 0600 o' clock, just before dawn, on 26 July. The 741st Tank Battalion, employing 18 medium tank rhinos, supported the 38th and 23d Infantry Combat Teams of the 2nd Infantry Division, while the 744th Light Tank Battalion using 54 light tank rhinos, supported the 9th Infantry Combat Team. The sortie was successful. The rhinos churned through the enemy to depths of 300 to 600 yards and returned without a single casualty due to enemy action. Interrogation of prisoners taken later indicated that the sortie had considerable shock power; the enemy was evidently unprepared for an onslaught of this type. In many instances the enemy, relying on the thick hedgerows for protection, were ground under the tanks as they smashed through hedgerow after hedgerow, while others were buried in their slit trenches or speared by the iron teeth of the rhino device. It was a bad time for the Nazis; their front lines were a shambles.

**D**

**_BOCAGE_-BUSTING DURING OPERATION _COBRA_**

A variety of tactics were adopted prior to Operation *Cobra*, with this example being typical. Two or more tanks fitted with Rhino hedgerow cutters were accompanied by at least one platoon of infantry. They would advance to the edge of a hedgerow and establish a base of fire against the opposite hedgerow. One of the tanks, such as the one here in the lower right, would find a clearing in one of the corners to provide overwatch and engage any German positions with its 75mm gun and machine guns. Once any German strongpoints were suppressed, a second tank would then charge through the hedgerow, clearing a path for the infantry. The infantry would then follow behind the tank. Once the field was secure, the process would be repeated.

Although the Rhino saw use for only a few days of combat, its employment had significant operational consequences because it facilitated the breakout from Normandy.

## Armored divisions in exploitation

From the standpoint of US armor doctrine, the primary role of the armored division was to utilize an infantry breakthrough to assault into the enemy rear and exploit the ensuing chaos and tactical opportunities. A textbook example was the conduct of Operation *Cobra* in July 1944 and the subsequent breakout from Normandy through August 1944.

Bradley's First US Army followed doctrine and kept the 2d and 3d Armored divisions in reserve from D-Day through mid-July 1944. A halfhearted attempt to reduce the Villiers-Fossard salient on June 29–30, 1944, by a combat command of the 3d Armored Division served to convince the First US Army to wait for a better opportunity to commit the armored divisions.

Operation *Cobra* was intended to exploit the growing weakness of the 7. Armee by penetrating the defensive line south of Saint-Lô to break out from the *bocage* country into the rear of the Wehrmacht in Normandy. The attack was launched on July 25 after heavy aerial bombardment of the German forward defenses. The initial VII Corps attack was conducted by three infantry defenses through a narrow corridor only about 5 miles wide. The infantry attacks were supported by separate tank battalions using the new Rhino hedgerow cutters. Although the plan had expected the first day's advance to reach 3 miles into German defenses, the attack only reached about 1 mile. The tactical doctrine was that armored divisions should not be unleashed until the infantry divisions had secured a clean breakthrough; but the VII Corps commander, Major General J. Lawton Collins, had fought the Wehrmacht long enough to know that the German Army reflexively launched counterattacks against enemy penetrations. The Germans had failed to stage any significant counterattack against the *Cobra* penetration, however, convincing Collins that he was facing a beaten enemy. Rather than wait, Collins ordered the 2d and 3d Armored divisions to begin to advance on July 26.

Besides the use of the Rhino hedgerow cutters, other tactical innovations were included in the Operation *Cobra* plan. Owing to the devastation inflicted by the preliminary aerial bombardment, Collins believed that the armored infantry battalions in halftracks could not keep up with the tanks. As a result, the assault waves had the infantry ride the tanks "Russian style." The 2d Armored Division was the more successful, pushing down two separate road nets with two combat commands abreast. The 2d Armored Division did not make extensive use of the Rhino devices, preferring to use roads when and where possible. By the night of June 28/29, the German forces in the sector had been enveloped into a pocket near the village of Roncey, further crushing German forces.

**E**

**CLOSE AIR SUPPORT TACTICS**

Direct air support for tank spearheads required a direct radio link between the fighter-bombers and the ground forces to prevent fratricide. This was first employed on a large scale during Operation *Cobra* in July 1944 with a tactic known as armored column cover. The US Army Air Forces provided an air–ground officer, usually a fighter pilot familiar with ground-attack tactics, who rode in a medium tank equipped with a special SCR-522 VHF radio to enable a direct radio link to the fighter aircraft. Without this critical link, the requests for air support had to be sent back to headquarters, and forwarded to the air units, complicating and delaying the process. This type of immediate air cover was not provided on a daily basis but was usually organized for specific important missions.

**LEFT**
One of the tactical innovations during the opening phases of Operation *Cobra* was to carry a squad of infantry aboard the tanks to facilitate tank/infantry cooperation. This is an M4 of Co. I, 33d Armored Regiment, 3d Armored Division, at the start of Operation *Cobra*. The tank was lost two weeks later when hit by German gunfire.

**RIGHT**
"Duke," an M4A1 (76mm) of Co. D, 66th Armored Regiment, CCA, 2d Armored Division, carries riflemen from the 22d Infantry, 4th Infantry Division, into action at the start of Operation *Cobra*.

By late July, Patton's Third US Army had arrived in France and was poised to amplify the Normandy breakout. On July 29, Patton's 4th and 6th Armored divisions began their attack down and along the coast toward Coutances and Avranches. German opposition was extremely weak. By the end of July, the First US Army had captured about 20,000 German troops and the 7. Armee was in full-scale retreat. The German theater commander, Generalfeldmarschall Günther von Kluge, warned Berlin that if Patton reached Avranches, "the Americans could do whatever they wished." The 4th Armored Division reached Avranches on July 31. Operation *Cobra* had secured not only a tactical breakthrough, but a full-scale operational breakout. Paris beckoned.

At this stage, Patton's Third US Army headed west into Brittany to secure vital ports while the First US Army headed east toward the Seine River and an envelopment of the German army in Normandy. The Brittany advance was the fastest to date with the 6th Armored Division reaching Brest in western Brittany and the 4th Armored Division reaching Lorient by August 7.

By this stage, the Allied high command had concluded that Patton's tanks were better employed racing eastward than westward, leaving the infantry to deal with the Breton ports. As a result, the First US Army continued a rapid exploitation toward the Seine with an aim to envelop the German army in Normandy from the south, while the Third US Army headed for the Seine near Paris. The fresh 7th Armored Division reached the cathedral city of Chartres on August 15, and the Third US Army crossed the Seine at Mantes north of Paris on August 20. The rapidity of this advance doomed the German army in Normandy.

Operation *Cobra* and the subsequent armored attacks by the First and Third US armies were textbook examples of the use of armored divisions in the exploitation of an infantry breakthrough.

## Tanks in urban combat

In World War II, the US Army lacked any detailed tactics for the use of tanks in urban fighting. FM 17-32 recommended: "Avoid villages if practicable. If the village must be taken, use infantry, engineers, mortars, and assault gun to attack frontally while tanks encircle the town." Towns and cities could constitute an improvised fortified zone, full of peril. Tanks were especially vulnerable to ambush by antitank guns and other antitank weapons within the close confines of an urban area. The presence of large numbers of civilians further complicated operations in built-up areas. The issue of urban combat was not formally addressed until 1979's FM 90-10 "Military Operations on Urbanized Terrain (Mounted)."

In the ETO, the US Army generally used infantry supported by tanks to capture cities. The first major urban fighting took place in late June 1944 during the liberation of the port of Cherbourg. There was subsequent fighting for other port cities such as Saint-Malo in Brittany, and Toulon and Marseilles in southern France. Most major French cities, including Paris, were abandoned by the Wehrmacht after limited resistance.

Arguably the most bitter urban battle in 1944 was the fight for the first German city of Aachen in October 1944. The US Army surrounded the city, and when the garrison refused to surrender, assaulted the city center during the second week of October 1944. Two battalions of the 1st Infantry Division's 26th Infantry Regiment were assigned the task of conducting the assault starting on October 12.

Lieutenant Colonel Derrill M. Daniel, commander of the 2/26th Infantry, coined the phrase for the improvised urban tactics – "Knock 'em all down" – that stressed the need to treat each urban structure as a fortified strongpoint that had to be overwhelmed before moving on to the next objective. These tactics stressed firepower over manpower. Each rifle company was organized as a task force with an attachment of three M4s of the 745th Tank Battalion or M10 tank destroyers of the 634th Tank Destroyer Battalion, two 57mm antitank guns, two bazooka teams, a flamethrower, and two heavy-machine-gun teams. The ultimate weapon was a 155mm M12 GMC lent by a self-propelled artillery battalion that was to be used to demolish any stubborn resistance with point-blank fire. To ensure that ammunition continued to flow in and casualties flow out in a timely fashion, Daniel obtained M29 Weasel tracked cargo carriers to deal with the rubble-filled streets. The tactics were to use firepower to chase the defenders into the cellars at which point they would be attacked with grenades and flamethrowers. The attack was staged to rout out the German defenders systematically, one street at a time. The infantry would move along the sides of the street, using the buildings for cover while the tanks and tank destroyers would move forward to provide direct firepower support. A week of savage fighting ensued, but Festung (Fortress) Aachen fell on October 21, 1944.

**LEFT**
M4A3 tanks and armored infantrymen of the 11th Armored Division cautiously advance through Andernach, Germany, on March 9, 1945, during efforts to clear out the pocket of the LXIII. Armeekorps troops trapped along the Rhine south of Remagen.

**RIGHT**
Troops of the 44th Armored Infantry Battalion accompany an M4A3(76mm HVSS) of Task Force 44, 6th Armored Division, in the town of Oberdorla, Germany, on April 4, 1945.

The employment of tanks to amplify field artillery was sometimes used in the ETO. Here, an enormous heap of 75mm ammunition transport containers have built up alongside an M4 being used to provide artillery fire support near Vicht, Germany, on November 17, 1944.

The single most savage urban battle fought by the US Army in World War II was the siege of Manila in the Philippines, dubbed "the Stalingrad of the Pacific." The fighting for Manila began in earnest during the second week of February 1945. The governmental district of the city was composed of modern earthquake-proof buildings constructed from steel-reinforced concrete. These were ideally suited for defensive purposes as was the old Spanish walled city of Intramuros. One tank-destroyer and two tank battalions took part in the urban battle for Manila. Their firepower proved invaluable in attacking Japanese strongholds. Nevertheless, the stout concrete buildings and the huge walls of Intramuros were resistant to 75mm gunfire. The assault-gun platoon of the 716th Tank Battalion was dispatched to Manila because the 105mm howitzers of the M4 assault guns were more effective in urban fighting than the usual 75mm tank guns. The 76mm gun of the M18 GMC of the 837th Tank Destroyer Battalion was found to be more effective due to its high velocity. The 105mm M7 HMC self-propelled howitzers of the infantry cannon companies were also widely used for attacking reinforced structures. The main threats to tanks in Manila were large-caliber guns, often taken from ships, as well as mines. Many of the mines were improvised from aircraft bombs and naval mines and so were unusually large and destructive. US casualties were over 1,000 dead and 5,500 wounded; Filipino civilian casualties were over 100,000 due to Japanese brutality. Few of the Japanese garrison of 16,000 survived.

**F**

**TANKS IN URBAN FIGHTING**

US tank doctrine did not encourage the use of tanks in urban areas due to the complexities of operating in narrow streets and the vulnerability of tanks to the growing numbers of German antitank rocket launchers. Nevertheless, urban combat was often inevitable, as is the case here in Cologne on March 5, 1945. Troops of the 415th Infantry, 104th Infantry Division, are shown during street fighting with the support of an M4(105mm) assault gun of HQ, Co. C, 750th Tank Battalion. The battalion's after-action report noted that "The operation continued into Cologne against very scattered resistance. The [Co. C] tanks supporting the 415th Infantry had slower going due mainly to blown overpasses and danger from dual-purpose [antiaircraft] guns. At the end of the day all the objectives had been taken easily and no [tank] losses sustained."

U.S.

An M4A3(76mm) of Co. C, 774th Tank Battalion, passes by a knocked-out Panther tank near Bovigny, Belgium, on January 12, 1945, while supporting the 83d Infantry Division in the final stages of the elimination of the "Bulge."

## Tank-vs-tank fighting

Although contemporary video tank games solely focus on tank-vs-tank combat, the US experience in the ETO was significantly different. Tank-vs-tank engagements were viewed as only one of a dozen major missions for the armored divisions. FM 17-100 listed it as number 10 of 12 missions and described it as: "Attacking to destroy enemy armored units when forced to do so as a matter of self-preservation or when hostile tanks threaten seriously to disrupt operations of other troops."

Tank-vs-tank combat in Normandy for the first six weeks was limited and usually involved small- scale encounters with German *Sturmgeschütz* assault guns and *Panzerjäger* tank destroyers. Panzer divisions did not begin to engage US forces until mid-July 1944, and not on the scale seen in the British sector around Caen. Although the 7. Armee lost over 100 Panzers in the Operation *Cobra* fighting, this was mainly due to encirclement actions and not direct tank-vs-tank confrontations. The first large-scale Panzer attack, Operation *Lüttich* near Mortain in early August 1944, was mainly fought against US infantry and artillery with modest involvement of US tanks.

The first large-scale tank-vs-tank fighting in the ETO involving US armored divisions was the German Panzer offensive in Lorraine in September 1944 against the Third US Army. This culminated in the fighting around Arracourt by the 4th Armored Division against elements of several German Panzer brigades. This was a meeting engagement with neither side enjoying any particular defensive advantage. Nevertheless, the battle was a decisive US tactical victory. While video tank games focus on technological factors as the fulcrum of victory, Arracourt was won due to the superior training and tactics of the US 4th Armored Division when facing inexperienced new German Panzer formations. By the end of the fighting, the 5. Panzerarmee had lost over 150 Panzers while the 4th Armored Division had lost 42 and controlled the battlefield.

**G**

**TANK-VS-TANK COMBAT**

Tank-vs-tank fighting in the ETO was usually sporadic and on a small scale until the Panzer offensive against the Third US Army in Lorraine in September 1944. The offensive involved the use of several of the new Panzer brigades that had been created in the summer of 1944. Although equipped with new Panther medium tanks, the brigades performed poorly in Lorraine due to poor organization, inexperience, and faulty command decisions. The culminating battles in the campaign centered on the town of Arracourt. The 4th Armored Division blunted the German attacks in a series of rolling tank battles, often fought in the early-morning hours in the fog. The Panther's advantage of impenetrable frontal armor was offset by the more experienced 4th Armored Division's M4 tank crews, who used the terrain to maneuver against the vulnerable sides of the German tanks, often at close range.

An M4A1 of Co. F, 33d Armored Regiment, CCB, 3d Armored Division, passes by a knocked-out PzKpfw IV Ausf G medium tank, probably from the 11. Panzer-Division, in Bad Marienberg on March 28, 1945, during the breakout from the Remagen bridgehead.

Tank-vs-tank fighting in the fall of 1944 was sporadic and on a small scale because the Panzer force had been gutted in Normandy. Hitler ordered the surviving Panzer force to be sequestered in reserve and rebuilt pending the forthcoming Ardennes offensive. There was a flare-up of fighting in November 1944 when the First US Army was conducting offensive actions toward the Roer River, threatening the staging areas of the Wehrmacht's Ardennes reserves. Hitler permitted some use of the Panzer reserves in these battles.

By far the largest tank-vs-tank battles fought by the US Army in the ETO were during the Ardennes campaign in December 1944–January 1945. The Wehrmacht's initial attack was conducted against four US infantry divisions supported by a very modest number of tanks. The initial German attack in the Ardennes on December 16 involved over 1,750 Panzers and AFVs. The US Army had over 4,000 M4s in the ETO, but in the Ardennes sector there were only three separate tank battalions with about 170 M4s, a ratio of about 10:1 in the Wehrmacht's favor. This imbalance was only transitory, however, as within hours of the start of the attack, the US Army began rushing armored divisions, separate tank battalions, and tank-destroyer battalions to the Ardennes.

The German advantages were fleeting and success depended on a rapid victory. The *Schwerpunkt* (focal point) of the offensive by the 1. SS-Panzerarmee in the northern sector failed when both the 1. SS-Panzer-Division and 12. SS-Panzer-Division suffered heavy losses and were stopped by determined infantry resistance backed by separate tank battalions.

The only German success was in the center sector when the 5. Panzerarmee successfully used infiltration tactics to overcome initial US infantry defenses, and then exploited the breakthrough with a Panzer advance to Bastogne. This happened too slowly to have an operational consequence, however. Owing to the time-consuming German pace, the US Army's VII Corps was able to counterattack with the heavy 2d and 3d Armored Divisions. Collins' VII Corps was very familiar with the operation of these nonstandard tank units and their relative imbalance of tanks over armored infantry. In order to amplify their combat power, Collins reinforced each of the armored divisions with an infantry regiment from neighboring infantry divisions, giving each the power of a small armored corps. The reinforced 2d Armored Division defeated the 5. Panzerarmee spearheads north of Bastogne in the days after Christmas and trapped a large number of Panzers in the Celles pocket. The reinforced 3d Armored Division fought a brutal series of battles with the II. SS-Panzerkorps on the approaches to the Tailles Plateau near Hotton and Manhay, halting their advance.

The US Army eventually deployed eight armored divisions during the Ardennes campaign. The Wehrmacht lost about 610 tanks and assault guns in the Ardennes, or about 45 percent of their original strength, compared to about 730 US tanks and tank destroyers, or about 20 percent of their armored strength.

Although not as well-known as the Ardennes campaign, Operation *Nordwind* saw Hitler attempt to exploit the distraction caused by the Ardennes offensive by staging a secondary offensive in Alsace. This involved some significant tank fighting by the inexperienced 12th and 14th Armored divisions in bloody battles near Herrlisheim and Rittershoffen in January 1945.

The heavy Panzer casualties suffered by the Wehrmacht in the December 1944–January 1945 offensives gutted the Panzer force in the West and it never recovered. At the beginning of February 1945, the Wehrmacht had only 1,162 Panzers operational in the West. By March 15, this had been reduced to 193 operational Panzers and assault guns and by April 10 to only 178. The main threats to Allied tanks in 1945 were towed antitank guns and the ubiquitous *Panzerfaust* antitank rocket launcher.

## Armored division combined-arms tactics

Armored divisions were organically structured for combined-arms operations. As mentioned previously, the 1943 TO&E had a balanced mixture of three tank battalions, three armored infantry battalions, and three armored field artillery battalions. The key to combined-arms tactics was the combat command, a brigade-type headquarters that could be allotted a mixture of these battalions depending on the mission. So, for example, a combat command could receive two tank battalions and one armored infantry battalion on a mission requiring speed and firepower, or one tank battalion and two armored infantry battalions on missions where greater

An M5A1 light tank of Co. A, 66th Armored, 2d Armored Division, shepherds an armored infantry battalion in the valley below near Buchet, northeastern France, August 31, 1944.

"Russian-style" tank riding became an increasingly popular tactic in the final months of the war as a means to build up the momentum of an advance. Here, troops of the 331st Infantry, 83d Infantry Division, ride on "El-Patty-Lou," an M4 of the 2d Armored Division, during the advance toward the Roer River on February 28, 1945.

infantry capability was needed such as in town fighting. In general, armored divisions usually employed two of their three combat commands at one time, keeping the third in reserve, hence the designation CCR for the third combat command.

The combat commands were structured for combined-arms tactics at battalion level. The US Army preferred to conduct combined-arms tactics at company level, however. As a result, combat commands usually operated with two or three task forces. The task force did not have a dedicated headquarters comparable to the combat command but rather used one of the battalion headquarters for this function. The accompanying chart shows the tactical structure of the 6th Armored Division during the fighting in Germany in early April 1945. As can be seen, the task forces in this division were numbered according to the battalion that served as the basis for the task force. In other divisions, it was common to use the name of the battalion commander rather than the number, for example Task Force Hogan, or Task Force Abrams. Other divisions made use of simple letter combinations such as TF X, TF Y, TF Z.

**H**

**COMBINED-ARMS TASK FORCE ATTACK**

A task force from an armored division's combat command could assign an integrated element to a specific mission, in this case, a team consisting of a platoon of armored infantry on halftracks and a supporting platoon of medium tanks. The assignment was the capture of a farmstead. The objective has already been brought under fire from an armored field artillery battalion, leading to fires in the farmstead. The field manuals advised against the use of halftracks with mounted infantry advancing against a defended objective. As a result, the halftracks have been parked as close to the objective as possible behind hedges along the row allowing the infantry to disembark under cover. The tank platoon has divided into two sections on either side of the road. The tanks remain outside *Panzerfaust* antitank rocket launcher range, a growing threat since the summer of 1944. The tanks fired smoke rounds and suppressing fire against the buildings and other likely targets before the farmstead was assaulted by the infantry. The illustration here shows the final stages of the combined-arms assault, with the dismounted infantry clearing the farmstead of any remaining German troops. The tank section on the far left has advanced closer to the farm buildings once the infantry has cleared any possible *Panzerfaust* teams hiding in the nearby hedges.

| Combat Command A, 6th Armored Division | | |
|---|---|---|
| **Task Force 15** | **Task Force 68** | **Task Force 9** |
| 15th Tank Bn. (-1 M4 co.) | 68th Tank Bn. (-1 M4, -1 M5 cos) | 9th Armored Infantry Bn. (-1 co.) |
| Armored infantry co. | Armored inf. co. | Medium tank co. |
| Tank destroyer plt. | Tank destroyer plt. | Tank destroyer plt. |
| Armored engineer plt. | Armored engineer plt. | Armored engineer plt. |
| 212th Armored Field Artillery Bn. | | 274th Armored Field Artillery Bn. |
| **Combat Command B, 6th Armored Division** | | |
| **Task Force 50** | **Task Force 69** | **Task Force 44** |
| 50th Armored Infantry Bn. (-1 co.) | 69th Tank Bn. (-1 M4 co.) | 44th Armored Infantry Bn. (-1 co.) |
| Medium tank co. | Armored inf. co. | Medium tank co. |
| Tank destroyer plt. | Tank destroyer plt. | Tank destroyer plt. |
| Armored engineer plt. | Armored engineer plt. | Armored engineer plt. |
| 231st Armored Field Artillery Bn. | 128th Armored Field Artillery Bn. | |

## Tank tactics in PTO amphibious landings

The US Army and US Marine Corps developed sophisticated and successful tactics for the employment of armor in support of amphibious landings in the PTO. One of the most significant differences from the ETO was the use of amphibious tanks (amtanks) to provide fire support during the landings.

The US Navy had pioneered the use of amphibious tractors (amtracs) in 1941 to help move troops and supplies ashore. The first of these, the Landing Vehicle Tracked (LVT-1), was used to transport supplies on Guadalcanal in 1942, Operation *Torch* in North Africa, and during the Aleutians campaign. The LVT-1 was followed by the more durable LVT-2 in 1942. The US Marine Corps began to consider using the amtracs in the assault phase of amphibious landings starting with the Tarawa landings in November 1943 because the amtracs could surmount coral reefs that would have stopped conventional landing craft.

Some consideration was given to producing an armed version of the amtrac as early as 1941. FMC Corporation used its new LVT-2 as the basis for an armed version fitted with the turret from the M3A3 and M5A1 light tanks with the rear radio bustle eliminated to save weight. The FMC LVT(A)-1 was

An LVT(A)-1 amtank supports troops of Co. A, 63d Infantry, 6th Infantry Division, during Operation *Globetrotter*, the amphibious landing near Sansapor, on the Vogelkop Peninsula of Middelburg Island in Dutch New Guinea (modern-day Indonesia) in August 1944.

A pair of LVT(A)-4 amtanks of the US Marine Corps' 2d Armored Amphibian Battalion in the first wave of landings on Iwo Jima on February 19, 1945.

selected in the summer of 1942, but due to a lack of priority, production did not begin until August 1943 with first deliveries in November 1943.

The US Marine Corps deployed the new amtanks in armored amphibian battalions. The first was formed in August 1943, followed by two more in 1943–44. The US Army had been following this program closely and joined in procurement of the LVT(A)-1 with 328 going to the Army and 182 to the Marine Corps by the time production ceased in February 1944. The Army raised its first amphibian tank battalion in October 1943. An Army amtank battalion consisted of an HQ company and service company and four amtank companies. Each company had 18 amtanks and two amtracs with the battalion possessing 75 of the former and 12 of the latter.

The combat debut of the LVT(A)-1 in the Marshall Islands in February 1944 made it clear that its 37mm M6 gun was inadequate to deal with typical Japanese fortified bunkers. In the meantime, the main Army amtrac training unit, the 18th Armored Group in Monterey, California, suggested the substitution of the turret of the 75mm M8 HMC. This change required minimal development effort beyond extending the superstructure to accommodate its wider turret race. The only downside to this change was that the two .30-caliber machine guns behind the turret had to be eliminated. Production of the LVT(A)-4 began in March 1944 and they were available for the campaign in the Mariana Islands in the summer of 1944. The LVT(A)-4 was used by both the Army and Marine Corps in the Pacific theater. No amtanks were ever deployed to the ETO. The Army received 1,307 LVT(A)-4s and the Marine Corps a further 533.

The Army and Marine Corps amtank battalions were used to spearhead an amphibious landing. Typically, a company of amtanks would constitute the first wave of a battalion landing team, followed by two waves of assault companies in amtracs. The amtanks delivered fire against shore targets on the approach to the beach and then provided fire support until the beach was secured by the infantry or Marines.

A pair of LVT(A)-1 amtanks of the US Army's 780th Amphibian Tank Battalion support infantry of the 96th Infantry Division near the Chatan landing site on Okinawa on April 1, 1945.

There was some controversy over tactics following the landings. The US Army doctrine was to have the amtanks remain on the beach after the landings on the presumption that they would be too vulnerable to conduct missions inland. The Marine Corps tactics initially encouraged the use of amtanks beyond the beachhead, but heavy casualties suffered during the Saipan landings in July 1944 led to a decision to restrict operations farther inland. Instead, the LVT(A)-4 was usually subordinated to the artillery after landings, because their 75mm howitzer was suitable for indirect-fire missions. Amtanks were often used in improvised roles. For example, during the Leyte campaign in the fall of 1944, Army amtanks would conduct amphibious missions offshore in support of infantry advances along the coast, serving as fire-support gunboats.

The PTO saw the extensive use of conventional tank battalions. The first major contested landing was on Tarawa Atoll in November 1943, conducted by Marine Corps M4A2 medium tanks. The tank landings were hampered by the lack of standardized deep-wading kits, however, and many tanks drowned in the surf. These problems had been largely remedied by the time of the landings in the Marshall Islands in February 1944, with Army and Marine Corps tanks receiving standardized deep-wading kits for the landings. Once the amtank battalions were available in 1944, the conventional tank battalions were landed in follow-on waves, usually from Landing Craft Mechanized (LCM). The role of the amtanks was to support the Army or Marine Corps in securing the beachhead while the conventional tank battalions were used to support the infantry in operations further inland.

The use of tanks in the PTO was very dependent on the varied terrain. Many of the objectives were islands and atolls covered in lush jungle with the terrain dominated by volcanic hills and mountains. In these circumstances, tanks were very limited in mobility. Other islands provided terrain more favorable to tank operations, however, such as the Marianas, the Philippines, and Okinawa. In these cases, there was extensive use of tanks for infantry support.

# LESSONS LEARNED

The US Army established boards and commissions to study combat lessons of armored units during the war. The first informal analysis of the organization of armored divisions was conducted by officers of Patton's Third US Army including Major General Robert W. Grow (6th Armored Division) and Major General Hugh J. Gaffey (4th Armored Division) in February 1945, with supplementary remarks by the former 4th Armored Division commander, Major General John P. Wood. These officers argued that the current divisions under the 1943 light TO&E were too small and required too many attachments. They preferred the 1942 "heavy" organization because it was more capable of powerful, sustained action. While acknowledging that the 1942 TO&E was imbalanced with too many tank battalions and not enough infantry, they argued in favor of more infantry rather than fewer tanks. Rather than continually attaching certain types of units such as antiaircraft battalions and medium field artillery battalions, the commanders recommended that they become organic to the division. This report helped form the basis for a study of the armored forces by the General Board that largely concurred with the February 1945 report.

The reorganized armored division of 1947 took these recommendations to heart, though it did not follow them precisely. Rather than increase the division to six battalions each of tank and infantry, a compromise was reached consisting of a division with four tank battalions including one heavy tank battalion, four armored infantry battalions, and four armored field artillery battalions including one 155mm heavy battalion.

In the case of the separate tank battalions, the main complaint of infantry commanders was that there was never enough tank support. There was broad unanimity that the tank battalions had to be made organic to the divisions and not a separate organization in order to foster better knowledge of the use of tanks by infantry officers and to facilitate training and cooperation between tanks and infantry. The postwar General Board recommended

The 75mm M8 howitzer motor carriage (HMC) was the light assault gun intended for light tank battalions. When the light tank battalions largely disappeared in 1943, the M8 HMC remained in service with US Army's mechanized cavalry units, such as this example in service with Troop E, 106th Cavalry Reconnaissance Group, near Karlsbrunn, Germany, on February 2, 1945.

In a scene reminiscent of World War II, a column of M26 Pershing medium tanks of 3-2d Armored Cavalry Regiment advance under the cover of a P-47 Thunderbolt of the 86th Fighter Wing during exercises near Eberbach, Germany, on April 21, 1949.

abandoning the attachment of one separate tank battalion to each infantry division, and instead to make a tank regiment organic to each division. The armored group concept was also abandoned as redundant.

The field manuals on tank tactics were gradually updated. One of the most influential tank officers after the war was Brigadier General Bruce C. Clarke. He served as a leader of CCA, 4th Armored Division, in the summer of 1944, and led CCB, 7th Armored Division, during its most notable battle at St. Vith in the Ardennes campaign in December 1944. After the war, while heading the Armored School at Fort Knox, Clarke described the tactical tenet of US tank units during and after the war: "There are certain basic principles which govern the employment of armor – but they are no more than guides. There is no place in the principles of armor for the words 'always' and 'never'. The successful application of the principles of armor employment is entirely dependent upon commanders and staffs being flexible in mind, progressive in thought, and liberal in imagination."

# FURTHER READING

There are surprisingly few books on US tank tactics in World War II. The most obvious source of information is the large number of wartime field manuals listed here, many of which can be found on the internet. The best guides to the changing tactics during the war are the reports of the Observer Boards that traveled to the battlefields to learn of new tactical developments. I used the set in the Ridgway Library at the US Army Heritage and Education Center, Carlisle, Pennsylvania. Each of the US Army higher headquarters had an Armored Section that advised the commander, and their reports can be found in Record Group 407 at the US National Archives and Records Administration, College Park, Maryland. Another valuable resource is the wartime and postwar articles on tank tactics in *Cavalry Journal/Armor Cavalry Journal*, digital copies of which can be found on the internet from the US Army Maneuver Center of Excellence, Fort Benning, Georgia.

## US Army Armored Field Manuals

FM 17-5, Armored Force Drill, January 1942; January 1943
FM 17-10, Tactics and Technique, March 1942
FM 17-12, Tank Gunnery, April 1943; July 1944
FM 17-15, Combat Practice Firing Armored Force Units, May 1942

FM 17-20, Employment of Armored Units Reconnaissance Platoon and Company, May 1942
FM 17-22, Reconnaissance Battalion, August 1942
FM 17-25, Assault Gun Section and Platoon, June 1942
FM 17-27, 81-mm Mortar Squad and Platoon, July 1942
FM 17-30, Tank Platoon, October 1942
FM 17-32, Tank Company, Light and Medium, August 1942
FM 17-33, The Armored Battalion, Light and Medium, September 1942
FM 17-34, Amphibious Tank and Tractor Battalions, June 1950
FM 17-36, Armored Employment of Tanks with Infantry, March 1944
FM 17-40, Armored Infantry Company, November 1944
FM 17-42, Armored Infantry Battalion, November 1944
FM 17-45, Armored Engineer Battalion, November 1942
FM 17-50, Logistics, November 1942
FM 17-55, Trains and Trains Headquarters Company Armored Division, September 1942
FM 17-57, Trains Company Armored Division, October 1942
FM 17-58, Armored Maintenance Battalion, Tactical Employment, October 1942
FM 17-59, Decontamination of Armored Force Vehicles, October 1942
FM 17-60, Armored Division Artillery, August 1942
FM 17-62, Fire Control and Coordination, July 1942
FM 17-63, Service of the Piece 105mm Howitzer Self-propelled, August 1942
FM 17-64, Service of the Piece 75-mm howitzer T-30 self-propelled, December 1942
FM 17-67, Crew Drill and Service of the Piece Medium Tank M4, August 1944
FM 17-68, Armored Crew Drill, Light Tank M5 Series, June 1943
FM 17-69, Crew Drill, Service of the Piece, and Gunnery (75-mm Assault Howitzer on Motor Carriage M8), November 1943
FM 17-70, Signal Communications for Armored Units, June 1944
FM 17-71, Crew Drill for Half-track Vehicles, September 1943
FM 17-74, Crew Drill and Service of the Piece, Heavy Tank, T25E1, August 1944
FM 17-75, Crew Drill, Light Tank, M24, August 1944
FM 17-76, Crew Drill and Service of the Piece, Medium Tank, M4 Series (105-mm Howitzer), September 1944
FM 17-80, Armored Medical Units, August 1944
FM 17-100, The Armored Division, January 1944

## US Army studies and reports

Anonymous (1943). *Report of Observers: Mediterranean Theater of Operations* (2 volumes). US Army Ground Forces Observer Board.
Anonymous (1944–45). *Report of Observers: European Theater of Operations*, (6 volumes). US Army Ground Forces Observer Board, 1944–45.
Anonymous (1945a). "Armored Section, First US Army, Annex 9," *First US Army Report of Operations.*
Anonymous (1945b). "Armored Section, 12th Army Group, Volume XI," *12th Army Group Report of Operations Final After Action Report.*
Anonymous (1945c). *Armored Fighting Vehicles and Weapons Section.* HQ, European Theater of Operations US Army.
Cameron, Robert S. (2008). *Mobility, Shock, and Firepower: The Emergence of the US Army's Armor Branch 1917–1945.* US Army Center of Military History.
Camp, T.J. (1943). *Tankers in Tunisia.* Fort Knox, KY: Armored Command.
Doubler, Michael (1988). *Busting the Bocage: American Combined Arms Operations in France: 6 June–31 July 1944.* Fort Leavenworth, KS: Combat Studies Institute.
Gott, Kendall (2006). *Breaking the Mold: Tanks in the Cities.* Fort Leavenworth, KS: Combat Studies Institute.

## Articles

Butler, James (1947). "Individual Tank-Infantry Communications," *Armored Cavalry Journal* 56.4: 43–45.
Larew, Karl (2005). "From Pigeons to Crystals: The Development of Radio Communications in US Army Tanks in World War II," *The Historian* 67.4: 664–77.

# INDEX

Figures in **bold** refer to illustrations and tables.